RAYS OF VICTORY SERIES

∞∞∞∞∞∞∞∞∞∞∞∞ ♦ ♦ ♦ ♦ ♦ ∞∞∞∞∞∞∞∞∞∞∞∞

RAYS OF VICTORY SERIES

∞∞∞∞∞∞∞∞∞ ♦ ♦ ♦ ♦ ♦ ∞∞∞∞∞∞∞∞∞

$\mathcal{T}$his Book Belongs to:

_____

(Your Beautiful Name)

Jesus Christ in you is Greater than the spirit of racism. Let His Footprints Lead you to daily Victory over racism.

RAYS OF VICTORY SERIES

∞∞∞∞∞∞∞∞∞∞ ♦ ♦ ♦ ♦ ♦ ∞∞∞∞∞∞∞∞∞∞

150 SIGN POSTS TO VICTORY OVER RACISM

(Volume 3)

Empowering Sign Posts for Victory Over Racism

∞∞∞∞∞∞∞∞∞ ♦ ♦ ♦ ♦ ♦ ∞∞∞∞∞∞∞∞∞

Excerpts from "Nailing Racism to the Cross" Cross"

∞∞∞∞∞∞∞∞∞∞ ♦ ♦ ♦ ♦ ♦ ∞∞∞∞∞∞∞∞∞∞

By
Dr. Jacyee Aniagolu-Johnson

First Paperback Edition

∞∞∞∞∞∞∞∞∞∞∞ ◆ ◆ ◆ ◆ ◆ ∞∞∞∞∞∞∞∞∞∞∞

"Racism is a contempt for life, an arrogant assertion that one race is the center of value and object of devotion, before which other races must kneel in submission."

– Rev. Dr. Martin Luther King, Jr.
(Civil Rights Leader)

∞∞∞∞∞∞∞∞∞∞∞ ◆ ◆ ◆ ◆ ◆ ∞∞∞∞∞∞∞∞∞∞∞

Volume 3

Edited by Chad Steenerson (www.christianeditor.net)
Also edited by Uché Aniagolu (Ebony WoodHouse Productions, LLC)

Editing Style:
Please note that the editing style presented in this book by the second editor, Uché Aniagolu, is meant to emphasize reverence of God, His Son Jesus Christ and His Holy Spirit. This editing style may differ from what you are accustomed to, but we chose it for the reason noted above.

Cover design by Marble Tower Publishing, LLC
Cover Image Source: Online Microsoft Clip Art Gallery (Open Source)

First Paperback Edition
ISBN 978-1-937230-03-6

Printed in the United States of America by Marble Tower Publishing, LLC

Publisher's Cataloging-In-Publication Data
(Prepared by The Donohue Group, Inc.)

Aniagolu-Johnson, Jacyee.

  150 sign posts to victory over racism : empowering sign posts for victory
over racism : excerpts from "Nailing racism to the cross" / Jacyee Aniagolu-
Johnson. -- 1st pbk. ed.

  3 v. ; cm. -- (Rays of victory series)

  ISBN: 978-1-937230-01-2 (v. 1)
  ISBN: 978-1-937230-02-9 (v. 2)
  ISBN: 978-1-937230-03-6 (v. 3)

  1. Racism--Religious aspects--Christianity. 2. Spiritual warfare. 3. Christian life. I. Title. II. Title: Nailing racism to the cross.

BV4599.5.R33 A56 2011
270/.08

∞∞∞∞∞∞∞∞∞ ◆ ◆ ◆ ◆ ◆ ∞∞∞∞∞∞∞∞∞

"The truth is that in the eyes of God, our race, ethnicity or nationality does not make us either superior or inferior to anyone or group of people. Our family lineage, education, wealth, social status, influence or any other factor or distinction, does not make us better than any other family; neither will anything we own or possess as individuals make us more acceptable to God than others. All men and women, regardless of race, ethnicity or nationality, are created equal in God's excellent Image, and in humanity and dignity. This is a simple and holy truth that racism can never change."

Jacyee Aniagolu-Johnson, PhD
(Excerpt from "Rays of Victory: Nailing Racism to the Cross")

∞∞∞∞∞∞∞∞∞ ◆ ◆ ◆ ◆ ◆ ∞∞∞∞∞∞∞∞∞

∞∞∞∞∞∞∞∞∞∞ ♦ ♦ ♦ ♦ ♦ ∞∞∞∞∞∞∞∞∞∞

Dedication

This book is dedicated to our heavenly Father, God Almighty—a God of justice, equity and all goodness enveloped in One—our only one and true living God, who offered us all the gift of eternal salvation through His Son, our Lord and Savior Jesus Christ.

To my dear father, Justice Anthony Aniagolu and my mother Maria Aniagolu whom I love dearly and who first taught me about God, His profound love, mercy, faithfulness and grace, and His holy justice against any form of evil, wickedness, oppression and injustice.

To all those, regardless of race or ethnicity, who need God's rays of victory to deal with and overcome racial prejudice and discrimination—may your individual victory through God's beams of justice come speedily as you abide in God's Holy Word and Presence through Jesus Christ.

∞∞∞∞∞∞∞∞∞∞ ♦ ♦ ♦ ♦ ♦ ∞∞∞∞∞∞∞∞∞∞

∞∞∞∞∞∞∞∞∞ ♦ ♦ ♦ ♦ ♦ ∞∞∞∞∞∞∞∞∞∞

Acknowledgement

My foremost gratitude is to God my heavenly Father for His Gift of Salvation through my Lord and Savior Jesus Christ, and His Holy Spirit Who dwells within me. It is He Who inspires and fuels me daily to overcome any and all challenges, including my experiences with racial prejudice and discrimination.

My deepest gratitude goes to my dad, Justice Anthony Aniagolu and my mom, Lady Maria Aniagolu, for being the most amazing parents and irreplaceable gifts from God. I will forever remain grateful to God for finding me worthy to have such phenomenal persons as mom and dad. I love always!

My special gratitude goes to my husband, Lamonte, who remains my earthly rock of Gibraltar, and through whom God continues to teach me His expression of true and unconditional love that has no bounds.

My special gratitude also goes to my sister, Maryanne, a lovely woman of God—thank you for continuing to help me to better understand how to hear the true voice of God and how to spend endless quality time in God's Holy Presence through prayer, thanksgiving and worship. I love you very much.

To my sister Uché, I thank God for the sweet fragrance of Christ in you. You are an embodiment of servanthood—selfless sacrificial giving, and it is the greatness of God in you through Jesus Christ that empowers you to humble yourself to serve others; I have no doubt that God will magnify His glory in your life through Jesus Christ. I love you very much.

To my sister Chi-Chi who's giving spirit surpasses any-one that I know—May Luke 6:38 remain like a wellspring within you and may God continue to bless you and enrich your life beyond your wildest imagination through Jesus Christ! I love you very much.

To my brother Kizito whose deep and genuine love for God helps me to stay focused on Matthew 6:33; may the power of God's Holy Word continue to promote you from faith to faith and from glory to glory, in the awesome Name of our Lord and Savior Jesus Christ. I love you very much.

To the rest of my family, Tony, Emeka, Chuka, Lolly and Nwachu, I remain forever grateful to God for your lives, individual families and accomplishments. It is my prayer that John 3:16 will be and remain alive in your hearts. I love you very much.

To my sisters in the Lord Jesus Christ, Chinwe Igwegbe-Lane and Nonye Igwegbe, thank you for all your prayers and support and powerful prophetic words that sustained me during the final birthing stage of the Rays of Victory book series. May our Heavenly Father continue to take you from faith to Faith and from glory to Glory, in the awesome Name of our Lord and Savior Jesus Christ!

To the rest my friends and prayer partners, and to the Body of Jesus Christ (believers in Christ—God's true priests and ministers around the world), regardless of denomination, race, ethnicity or nationality, may God's favor and blessings always overflow in your lives as you continue to spread the good news of the Gospel of our Lord and Savior Jesus Christ, and further His powerful ministry, all of which are firmly rooted in true and pure love, which is God Himself.

Contents

∞∞∞∞∞∞∞∞∞∞ ◆ ◆ ◆ ◆ ◆ ∞∞∞∞∞∞∞∞∞∞

What is Racism?

"A situation in which one race maintains supremacy over an-other race through a set of attitudes, behaviors, social structures and ideologies. It involves four essential and interconnected ele-ments:

Power: *the capacity to make and enforce decisions is dispro-portionately or unfairly distributed.*

Resources: *unequal access to such resources as money, educa-tion, information, etc.*

Standards: *standards for appropriate behavior are ethnocen-tric, reflecting and privileging the norms and values of the dominant race/society.*

Problem: *involves defining "reality" by naming "the problem" incorrectly, and thus misplacing it."*

*-- **Women's Theological Center, Boston, MA, 1994***

∞∞∞∞∞∞∞∞∞∞ ◆ ◆ ◆ ◆ ◆ ∞∞∞∞∞∞∞∞∞∞

∞∞∞∞∞∞∞∞∞ ♦ ♦ ♦ ♦ ♦ ∞∞∞∞∞∞∞∞∞

Definitions of Racism

"Any distinction, exclusion, restriction, or preference based on race, color, descent, or national or ethnic origin which has the purpose or effect of nullifying or impairing the recognition, enjoyment, or exercise, on equal footing, of human rights and fundamental freedoms in the political, economic, social, cultural, or any other field of public life."

-- The ICERD (International Convention on the Elimination of All Forms of Racial Discrimination)

∞∞∞∞∞∞∞∞∞ ♦ ♦ ♦ ♦ ♦ ∞∞∞∞∞∞∞∞∞

"Racism has not disappeared… we confront forms of racism that are covert or more complex…"

-- The International Council on Human Rights Policy

∞∞∞∞∞∞∞∞∞ ♦ ♦ ♦ ♦ ♦ ∞∞∞∞∞∞∞∞∞

"Racism involves physical, psychological, spiritual, and social control, exploitation and subjection of one race by another race…This means that racial discrimination and injustice are established, perpetuated and promoted throughout every institution of society - economics, education, entertainment, family, labor, law, politics, religion, science and war…"

-- Phavia Kujichagulia

(Recognizing and Resolving Racism: A Resource and Guide for Humane Beings)

∞∞∞∞∞∞∞∞∞∞ ♦ ♦ ♦ ♦ ♦ ∞∞∞∞∞∞∞∞∞∞

"Racism - Racial prejudice and discrimination that are supported by institutional power and authority. The critical element that differentiates racism from prejudice and discrimination is the use of institutional power and authority to support prejudices and enforce discriminatory behaviors in systematic ways with far-reaching outcomes and effects..."

-- Enid Lee, Deborah Menkart and Margo Okazawa-Rey (eds.)
(Beyond Heroes and Holidays: A Practical Guide to K-12 Anti-Racist, Multicultural Education and Staff Development.)

∞∞∞∞∞∞∞∞∞∞ ♦ ♦ ♦ ♦ ♦ ∞∞∞∞∞∞∞∞∞∞

∞∞∞∞∞∞∞∞∞ ♦ ♦ ♦ ♦ ♦ ∞∞∞∞∞∞∞∞∞

The Reason for this Book

For every person, every child of God to know, understand and use the awesome power of God's Holy Word and His power within him or her through Jesus Christ to slay the goliath racism that they may encounter anywhere.

"You, dear children, are from God and have overcome them, because the one who is in you is greater than the one who is in the world."
– 1 John 4:4, NIV

∞∞∞∞∞∞∞∞∞∞ ♦ ♦ ♦ ♦ ♦ ∞∞∞∞∞∞∞∞∞∞

To receive the spirit of racism is to reject God's Holy Word.
To practice racism is to disobey God's Holy Word.
To reject the spirit of racism is to uphold God's Holy Word.

∞∞∞∞∞∞∞∞∞∞ ♦ ♦ ♦ ♦ ♦ ∞∞∞∞∞∞∞∞∞∞

∞∞∞∞∞∞∞∞∞∞ ♦ ♦ ♦ ♦ ♦ ∞∞∞∞∞∞∞∞∞∞

Preface

This book, "150 Sign Posts to Victory Over Racism-Volume 3," is a continuation of Volume 2 containing excerpts from the "Rays of Victory-Nailing Racism to the Cross" series.

The goal in writing this book is to lead you to accept Jesus Christ as your personal Lord and Savior, if you have not already done so; to guide you to God's holy truth in His Holy Word by the revelation power of His Holy Spirit; and for you to understand how to submit to God's Word and allow Him to unveil your natural eyes, replacing them with spiritual eyes through Jesus Christ.

With spiritual eyes you can begin to recognize the activities of the foul spirit of racism that is behind the racial prejudice and discrimination that you have experienced in the past or that you are currently experiencing. You will come to understand how racism attacks you and tries to intimidate you to submit to evil domination.

With a spiritual mindset, you will understand how to resist and defeat the obnoxious spirit of racism with God's Holy Word, the Sword of the Spirit. You will also understand how to be used as an instrument of God, transformed to His "battleaxe" against all demonic influences through Jesus Christ

(Ephesians 6:17; Jeremiah 51:20-23). God's Holy Word loaded in you fortifies and transforms you into His battleaxe, a spiritual prayer warrior against all forms of evil, including racism (Psalms 144:1-2). As God's battleaxe you cannot be a human receptacle for the evil spirit of racism or its tool for perpetrating racism, or see yourself as a victim of racism; rather you are a victorious spiritual warrior over racism through Jesus Christ.

The world tells us to "Fake it till we make it"; but God's tells us in His Word to "Faith it" till we make it. (Hebrews 11:1; Hebrews 10:35) This is the conquering power of our faith in Him through Jesus Christ (Romans 8:37). If racism is against you, you must believe that through Christ you have victory over evil, including racism (1 John 4:4, 5:44).

The excerpts in this book are about showing you how not to submit to the obnoxious spirit of racism; rather how to apply God's Holy Word by your faith to demolish the stranglehold that racism may have on your soul—your heart, mind, thoughts, will, and resolve, and also on your personality, actions, and behavior. If you have already allowed the foul spirit of racism access to your soul, now is the time to cast it out. If you have not granted the evil spirit of racism any such access, keep the door to your soul permanently shut to it, with the power of the holy truth of God's awesome Word.

The truth is that our race or ethnicity does not make us either superior or inferior to anyone or group. Therefore, in the awesome Name of our Lord and Savior Jesus Christ: Reject racism! Rebuke racism! Bind the foul spirit of racism!—and receive your victory in Jesus Christ over the loathsome spirit of racism and its evil product racism.

∞∞∞∞∞∞∞∞ ♦ ♦ ♦ ♦ ♦ ∞∞∞∞∞∞∞∞
Scripture Meditation

Let God battle those who oppress you—let God oppose those who oppose you—let Him be an Enemy to your enemies and an Adversary to your adversaries (Exodus 23:22)—let Him gain victory for you—the battle is not yours but the Lords'

– 1 Samuel 17:45-47

∞∞∞∞∞∞∞∞ ♦ ♦ ♦ ♦ ♦ ∞∞∞∞∞∞∞∞

∞∞∞∞∞∞∞∞ ♦ ♦ ♦ ♦ ♦ ∞∞∞∞∞∞∞∞

How to Use this Book

This book, "150 Sign Posts to Victory Over Racism- Volume 3," contains excerpts from the "Rays of Victory Series – Nailing Racism to the Cross,"empowering guideposts for victory over racism. During your quiet and serene moments, read and meditate on each excerpt, page by page, and most importantly, on God's Holy Word. Let it soak your heart and mind and help you to begin to carve out a spiritual roadmap for you as your daily Christ-rooted strategy for victory over racism. Let each excerpt help you to refocus your mind on God's Holy Word and its holy power to renew and fortify your mind against the foul spirit of racism (Romans 12:2).

Are you burdened by the foul spirit of racism and cannot seem to shake it off? Do you wish to turn over a new leaf with a life that is devoid of prejudiced feelings or racist actions? Are you a member of the huge "club" of individuals who face the daily storms of racism in the workplace or elsewhere? Have you had enough of the negative spiritual, mental or even physical abuse and torture by your experiences with racism? If you have, please come with me on this powerful trip with God's Spiritual knowledge, guidance and empowerment. Let the excerpts in is book, empowering "sign posts" guide you on how to draw daily-renewed strength from God's Holy Scripture. Let the power of God's Holy Word and His amazing grace un-shackle you forever from the invisible chains of racism.

First, let's profess Jesus Christ as our Lord and Savior, and receive the redeeming power of His precious Blood in our individual lives. For it is under the covering of the precious Blood of Jesus that we can receive the hidden power of God's Rays of Victory over racism (Habakkuk 3:4).

∞∞∞∞∞∞∞∞∞∞ ♦ ♦ ♦ ♦ ∞∞∞∞∞∞∞∞∞∞

∞∞∞∞∞∞∞∞∞∞ ♦ ♦ ♦ ♦ ♦ ∞∞∞∞∞∞∞∞∞∞

A Prayer of Salvation

On this day, _____, I, _____ confess with my mouth that the Lord Jesus Christ is my personal Savior; I believe that He shed His Blood for me on the Cross of Calvary and that God raised Him from the dead for my eternal salvation. I repent of my sins and ask God for forgiveness through the mighty Blood of Jesus Christ.

On this day, _____ by my faith, I, _____ believe that I am now saved by the precious Blood of Jesus Christ. I believe in the Triune God: God the Father, God's Son, Jesus Christ and God the Holy Spirit. I believe that in the Name of our Lord and Savior JesusChrist, I will receive the baptism of God's Holy Spirit that will release from my heart the flowing rivers of Living Water, in Jesus' Name, Amen.

Thank you Father, Lord God, for on this day, _____, in the Name of Jesus Christ, I, _____ am Born Again!

Scripture Meditation:

"For God so loved the world that He gave His Only Begotten Son, that whoever believes in Him should not perish but have everlasting life."
— John 3:16

"But what does it say? 'The word is near you, in your mouth and in your heart' (that is, the word of faith which we preach): that if you confess with your mouth the Lord Jesus and believe in your heart that God has raised Him from the dead, you will be saved. For with the heart one believes unto righteousness, and with the mouth confession is made unto salvation."
— Romans 10:8-9

"He who believes in Me, as the Scripture has said, out of his heart will flow rivers of Living Water."
— John 7:38

"That which is born of the flesh is flesh, and that which is born of The Spirit is spirit. Do not marvel that I said to you, 'You must be Born Again.'"
— John 3:6-7

Prayer after Profession of Salvation

∞∞∞∞∞∞∞∞∞ ♦ ♦ ♦ ♦ ♦ ∞∞∞∞∞∞∞∞∞

Dear Glorious Heavenly Father, thank You that I am born again by the precious Blood of Jesus Christ. I accept my renewed spirit in Him.

Dear gracious Father, I thank You for making me aware that I have spiritual and mental shackles from my experiences with racism. Thank You for revealing to me all areas where I am shackled. Thank You for giving me total release and freedom from the intrigues of the foul spirit of racism. I reject the evil tradition of racism and all that it stands for. I forgive anyone who has hurt or offended me in any manner, including my racist offenders.

Dear precious Father, I believe that You have answered my prayers in the precious Name of Jesus Christ. In the Name of Christ and by Your enabling grace, Lord God, I know that I can and that I have gained victory over any form of racial oppression and injustice.

Thank You, awesome Father, for Your marvelous rays of victory over racism on my behalf, and for Your limitless and boundless power within me through Jesus Christ, Amen.

Scripture Meditation:

"And whatever you ask in My Name, I will do, that the Father may be Glorified in the Son. If you ask anything in My Name, I will do it."
— John 14:13-14

"Pray without ceasing; in everything give thanks; for this is the Will of God in Jesus Christ for you."
— 1 Thessalonians 5:17-18

"And whenever you stand praying, if you have anything against anyone, forgive him that your Father in Heaven may also forgive you your   trespasses."
— Mark 11:25

"Until now you have asked nothing in My Name. Ask and you will receive, that your joy may be full."
— John 16:24

"Don't copy the behavior and customs of this world, but let God transform you into a new person by changing the way you think. Then you will learn to know God's Will for you, which is good and pleasing and perfect."
— Romans 12:2

∞∞∞∞∞∞∞∞∞ ♦ ♦ ♦ ♦ ∞∞∞∞∞∞∞∞∞

Partnership Prayer

∞∞∞∞∞∞∞∞∞ ♦ ♦ ♦ ♦ ∞∞∞∞∞∞∞∞∞
♥

I commit to spending quality time in prayer, worship and thanksgiving, and meditating on God's Holy Word, to receive His powerful and winning strategies for my daily victory over racism. This I shall do only by the grace of God, in the Name of our Lord and Savior Jesus Christ and through daily guidance by the Holy Spirit. I stand in agreement with my prayer partner(s) _____ believing that through the redeeming precious Blood of Jesus Christ, God has taken away the burden of racism, its reproach and yoke of destruction from all areas of my life. I stand in agreement with my prayer partner(s) _____ believing that the precious Blood of Jesus Christ has permanently destroyed and removed the power of the burden of the foul spirit of racism in my life, in Jesus' Name, Amen.

_____
Your Name

_____
Prayer Partner's Name

∞∞∞∞∞∞∞∞∞ ♦ ♦ ♦ ♦ ∞∞∞∞∞∞∞∞∞

Jacyee Aniagolu Johnson

Dr. Jacyee Aniagolu-Johnson
(Author remains in agreement with you)

"Again I say to you that if two of you agree on earth concerning anything that they ask, it will be done for them by My Father in heaven." – Matthew 18:19

"It shall come to pass in that day that his burden will be taken away from your shoulder, and his yoke from your neck, and the yoke will be destroyed because of the anointing oil." – Isaiah 10:27

♥

∞∞∞∞∞∞∞∞∞ ♦ ♦ ♦ ♦ ∞∞∞∞∞∞∞∞∞

Introduction

∞∞∞∞∞∞∞∞∞∞ ♦ ♦ ♦ ♦ ♦ ∞∞∞∞∞∞∞∞∞∞

This book, "150 Sign Posts to Victory Over Racism-Volume 3," will lead you to God's Holy Word, the Holy Bible, and show you how the power of God's Word can help you to gain individual victory over racism—when you stand in the victory that Jesus Christ gained for you on the Holy Cross (1 John 5:4), where He nailed your sins and every form of evil, wickedness, repression or oppression, including racism (Colossians 2:14).

To stand in victory over racism, you must come first under the covering of the precious Blood of our Lord and Savior Jesus Christ (John 3:6,16, Romans 10:9-10). If you confess with your mouth the Lord Jesus and accept in your heart that God raised Him from the dead, you will be saved. This means that you will be born again—transformed into a new spiritual creation in Christ (2 Corinthians 5:17; Galatians 2:20; Romans 10:9-10). What does it mean to become "born again" in Jesus Christ? To be "born again" or "reborn" in Jesus Christ does not mean a physical rebirth but a spiritual renewal of your spirit.

To gain individual victory over racism or any other form of evil, you must first come to know and understand who you are in Jesus Christ. You are a child of God through the right-eousness of Jesus Christ, an heir of God, and joint-heir with Christ (Romans 8:15-18). You are fearfully and wonderfully made, an excellent product of His marvelous works (Psalms 139:13-14). So, you must come to see yourself as God sees you and not as prejudiced or racist individuals see you or present you to the world. You must allow God's Holy Word to renew your mind through Jesus Christ (Romans 12:2) so that you do not allow racism to distort your view or perception of your im-age of yourself.

Have you already allowed racism to distort your dis-cernment of your true image of yourself in your mind? If you have, please allow the power of God's Holy Word in the Name of Jesus Christ to start the process of renewing your mind and give you a brand new view of your true image which is your au-thentic spiritual self-image in Him.

As a child of the Most High God, you cannot allow the foul spirit of racism to deceive you into believing the lies that racism presents to you about who you are. You are to believe God's Word and obey His Word and do His will (James 1:22-25). God's will is for you to silence the foul spirit of racism with the power of His Holy Word in you. You are what God's Word says you are and not what racism declares that you are. As a child of God you have His power in you—His Holy Spirit in you through Jesus Christ—to pull down every stranglehold or iron grip of racism, and bring racism and its evils to submit to

God's Holy Word (2 Corinthians 10:3-5). Through Christ, let us follow God's holy "sign posts" to victory over racism. Let's begin!

"150 Sign Posts to Victory Over Racism – Volume 3" Begins:

1

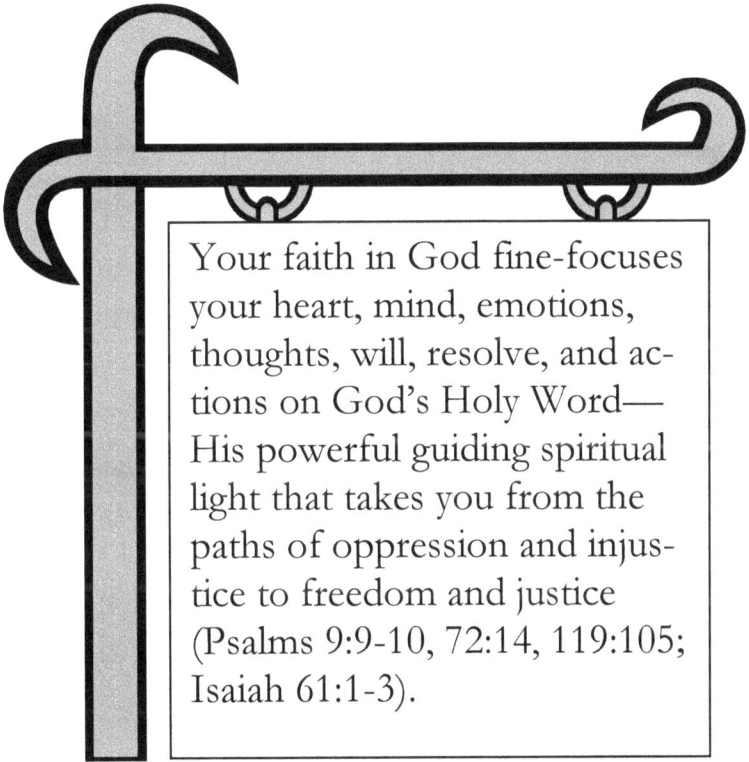

Your faith in God fine-focuses your heart, mind, emotions, thoughts, will, resolve, and actions on God's Holy Word— His powerful guiding spiritual light that takes you from the paths of oppression and injustice to freedom and justice (Psalms 9:9-10, 72:14, 119:105; Isaiah 61:1-3).

2

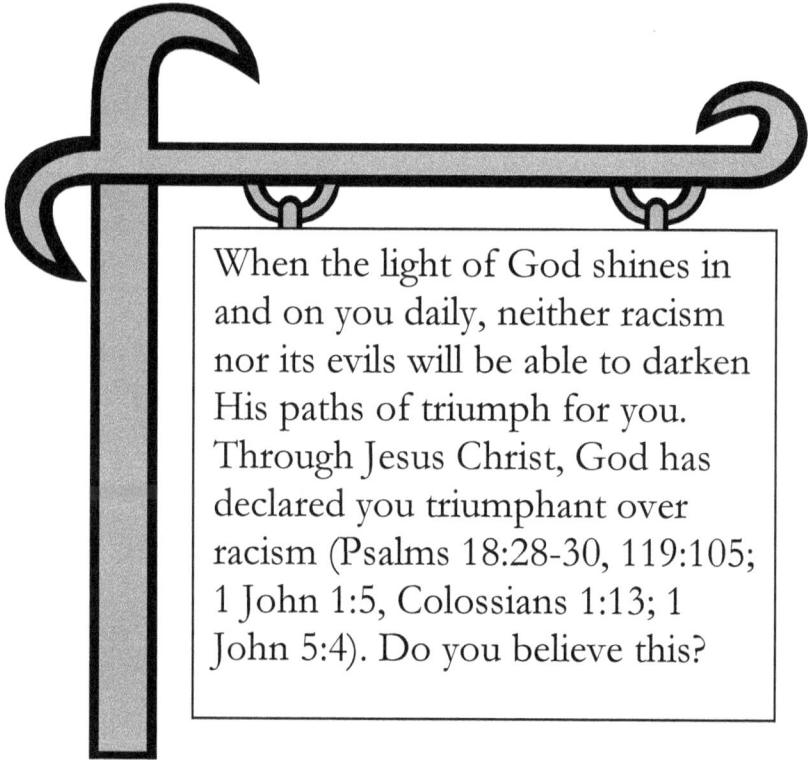

When the light of God shines in and on you daily, neither racism nor its evils will be able to darken His paths of triumph for you. Through Jesus Christ, God has declared you triumphant over racism (Psalms 18:28-30, 119:105; 1 John 1:5, Colossians 1:13; 1 John 5:4). Do you believe this?

3

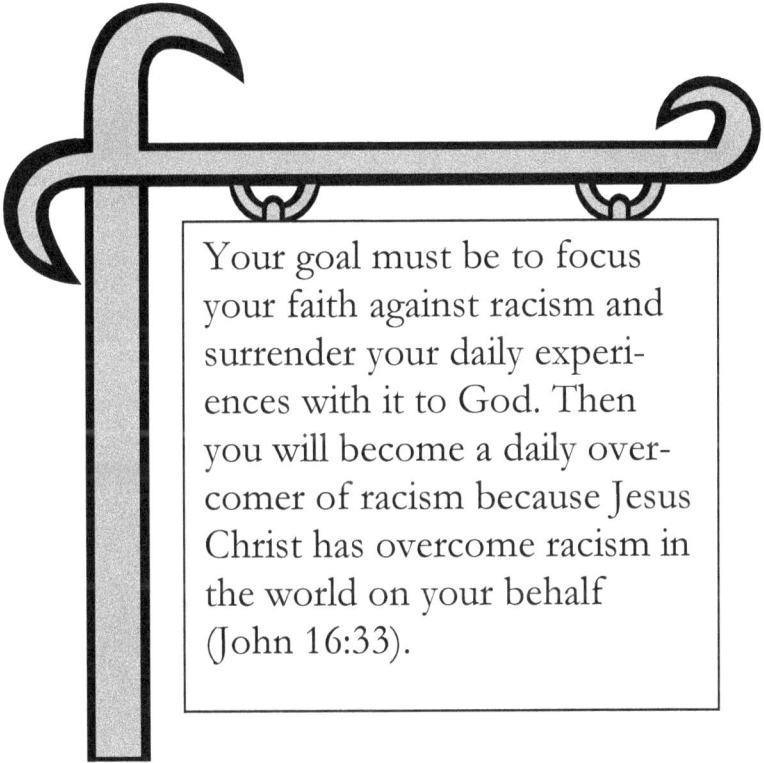

Your goal must be to focus your faith against racism and surrender your daily experiences with it to God. Then you will become a daily overcomer of racism because Jesus Christ has overcome racism in the world on your behalf (John 16:33).

4

Against the foul spirit of racism, you shall declare: *"For You will light my lamp; the Lord my God will enlighten my darkness. For by You I can run against a troop, by my God I can leap over a wall. As for God, His way is perfect; the word of the Lord is proven; He is a shield to all who trust in Him" (Psalms 18:28-30 NKJV).*

5

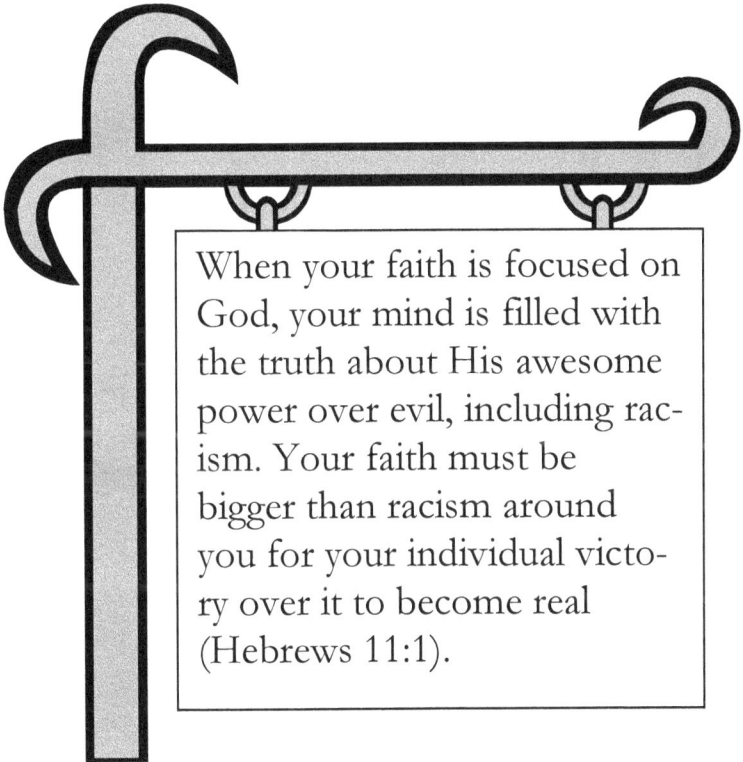

When your faith is focused on God, your mind is filled with the truth about His awesome power over evil, including racism. Your faith must be bigger than racism around you for your individual victory over it to become real (Hebrews 11:1).

6

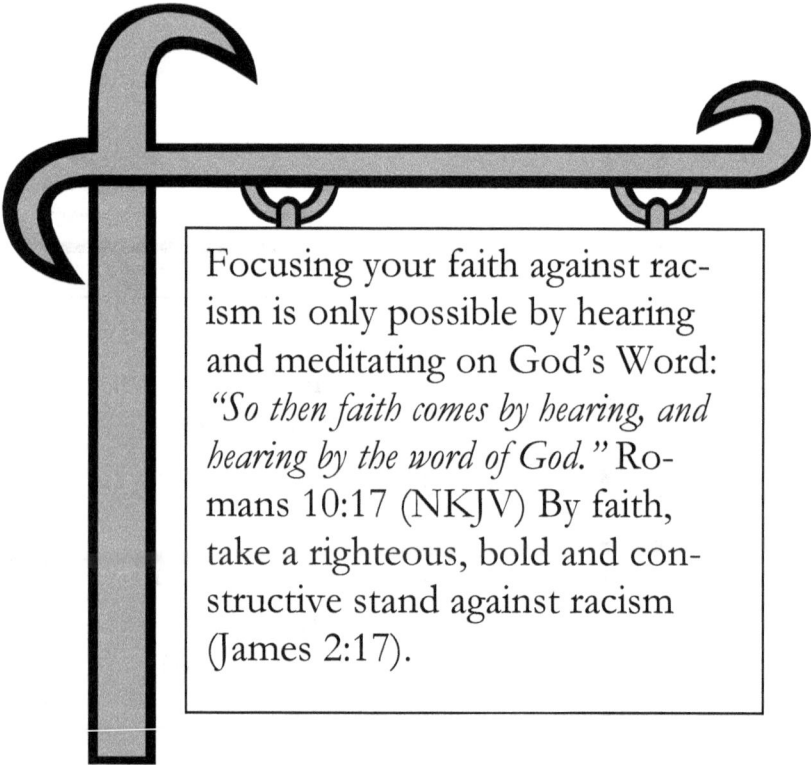

Focusing your faith against racism is only possible by hearing and meditating on God's Word: *"So then faith comes by hearing, and hearing by the word of God."* Romans 10:17 (NKJV) By faith, take a righteous, bold and constructive stand against racism (James 2:17).

7

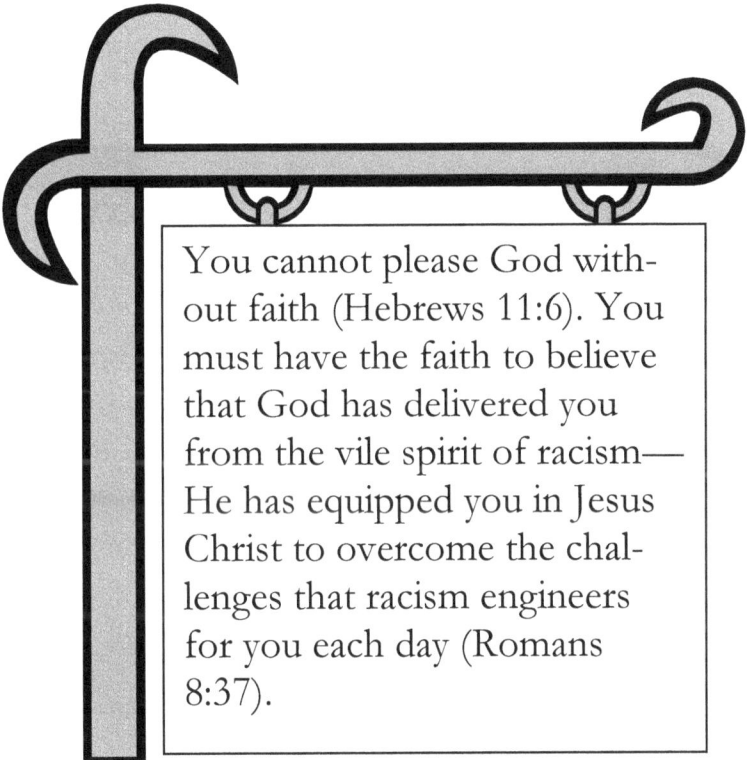

You cannot please God without faith (Hebrews 11:6). You must have the faith to believe that God has delivered you from the vile spirit of racism— He has equipped you in Jesus Christ to overcome the challenges that racism engineers for you each day (Romans 8:37).

8

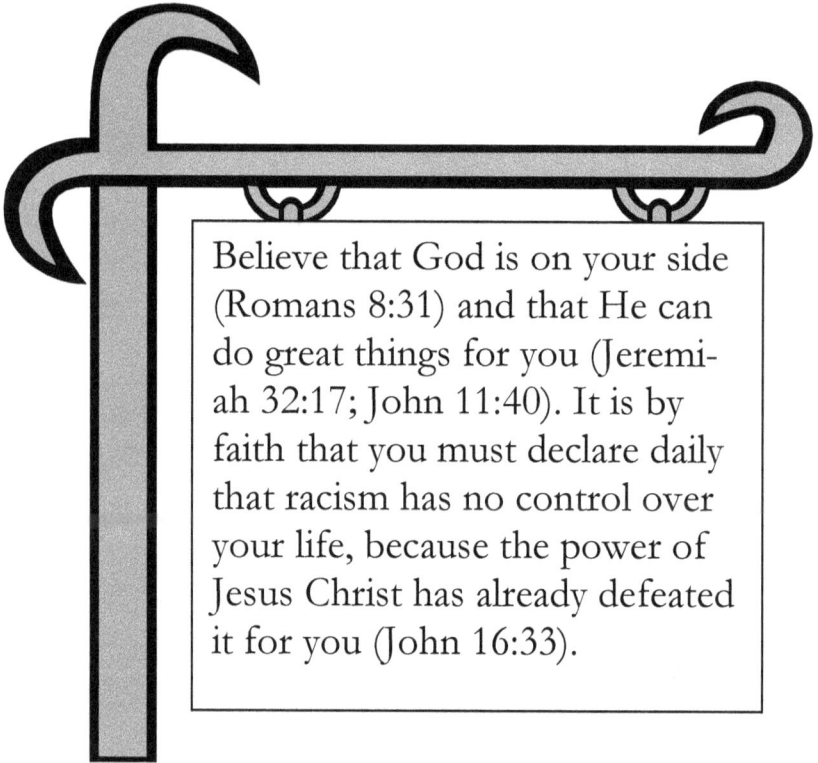

Believe that God is on your side (Romans 8:31) and that He can do great things for you (Jeremiah 32:17; John 11:40). It is by faith that you must declare daily that racism has no control over your life, because the power of Jesus Christ has already defeated it for you (John 16:33).

9

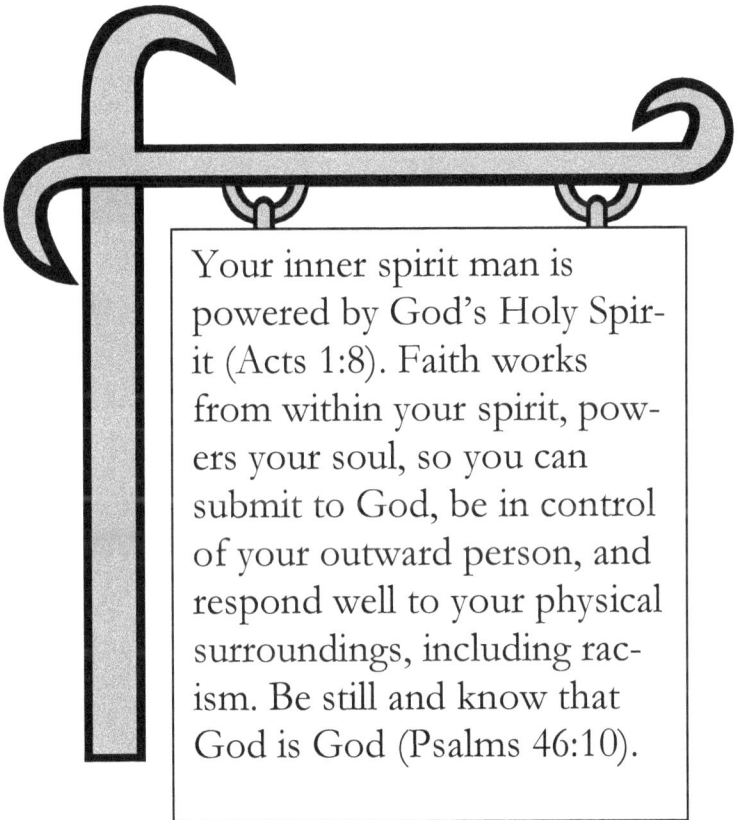

Your inner spirit man is powered by God's Holy Spirit (Acts 1:8). Faith works from within your spirit, powers your soul, so you can submit to God, be in control of your outward person, and respond well to your physical surroundings, including racism. Be still and know that God is God (Psalms 46:10).

10

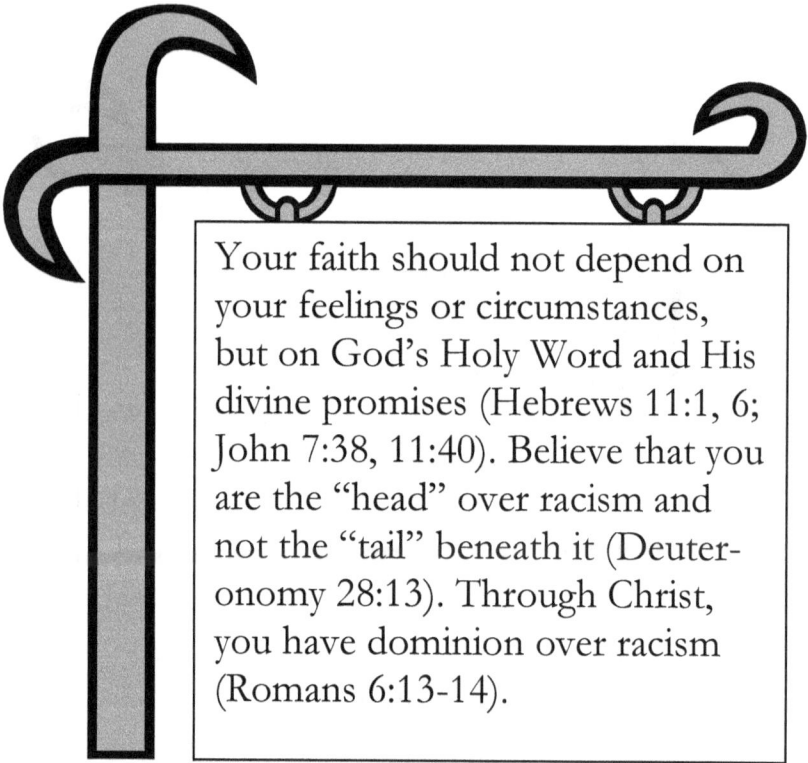

Your faith should not depend on your feelings or circumstances, but on God's Holy Word and His divine promises (Hebrews 11:1, 6; John 7:38, 11:40). Believe that you are the "head" over racism and not the "tail" beneath it (Deuteronomy 28:13). Through Christ, you have dominion over racism (Romans 6:13-14).

11

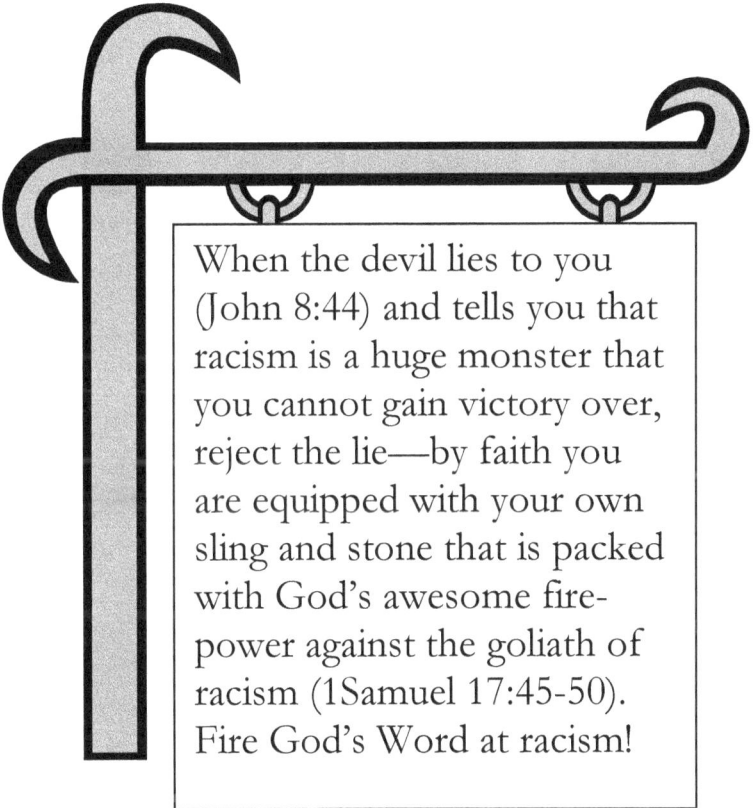

When the devil lies to you (John 8:44) and tells you that racism is a huge monster that you cannot gain victory over, reject the lie—by faith you are equipped with your own sling and stone that is packed with God's awesome fire-power against the goliath of racism (1Samuel 17:45-50). Fire God's Word at racism!

12

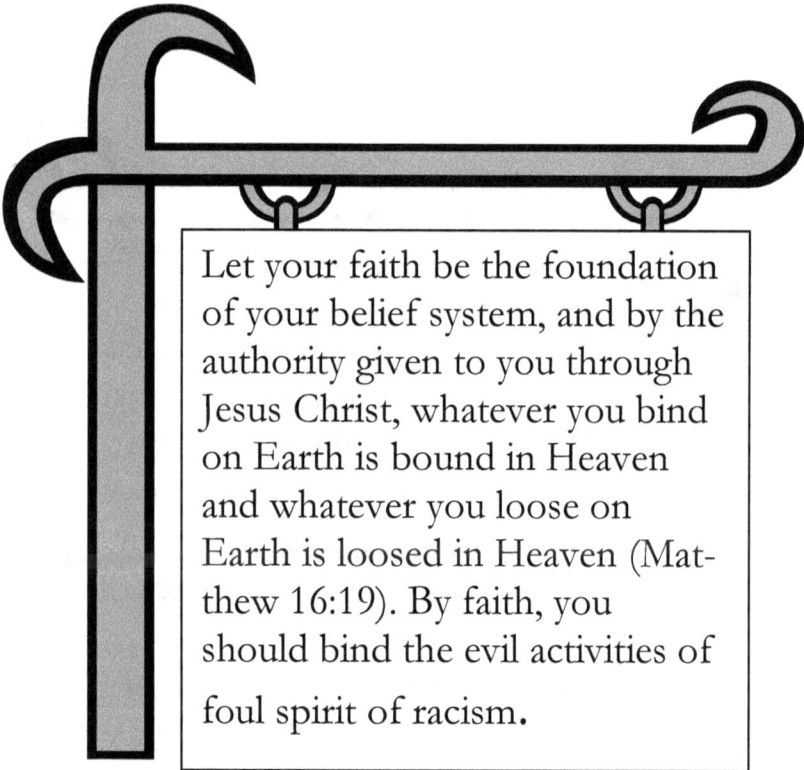

Let your faith be the foundation of your belief system, and by the authority given to you through Jesus Christ, whatever you bind on Earth is bound in Heaven and whatever you loose on Earth is loosed in Heaven (Matthew 16:19). By faith, you should bind the evil activities of foul spirit of racism.

13

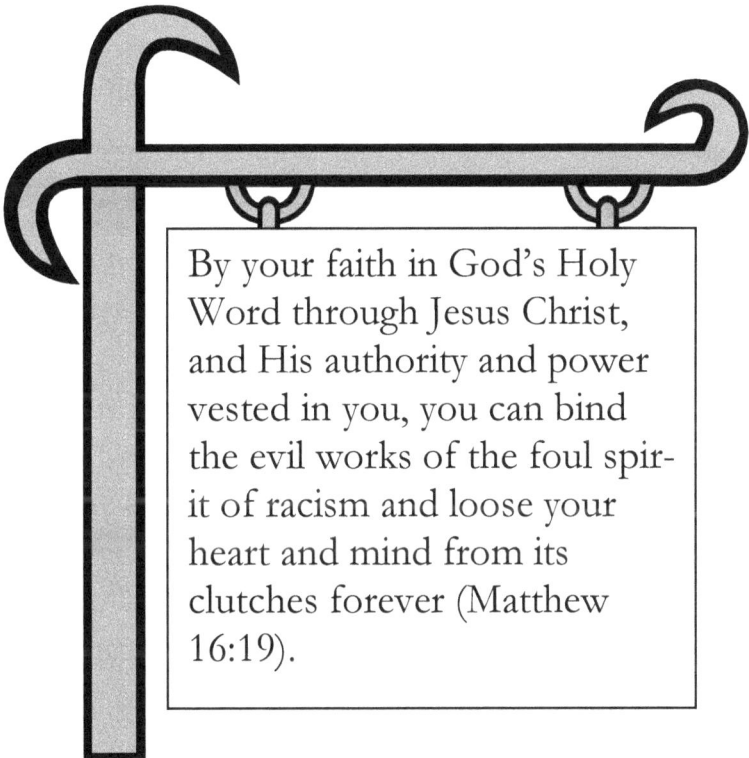

By your faith in God's Holy Word through Jesus Christ, and His authority and power vested in you, you can bind the evil works of the foul spirit of racism and loose your heart and mind from its clutches forever (Matthew 16:19).

14

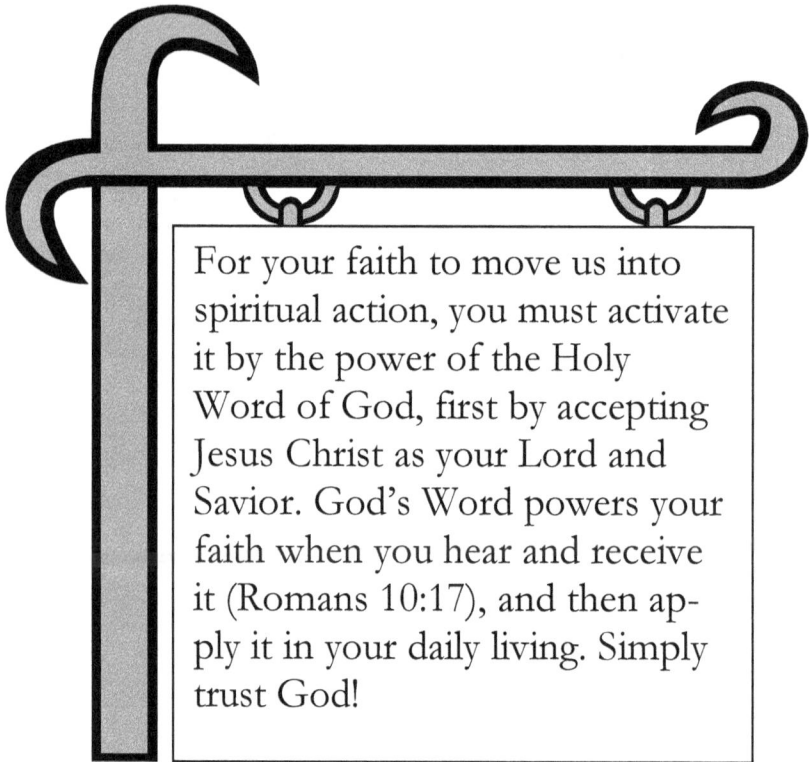

For your faith to move us into spiritual action, you must activate it by the power of the Holy Word of God, first by accepting Jesus Christ as your Lord and Savior. God's Word powers your faith when you hear and receive it (Romans 10:17), and then apply it in your daily living. Simply trust God!

15

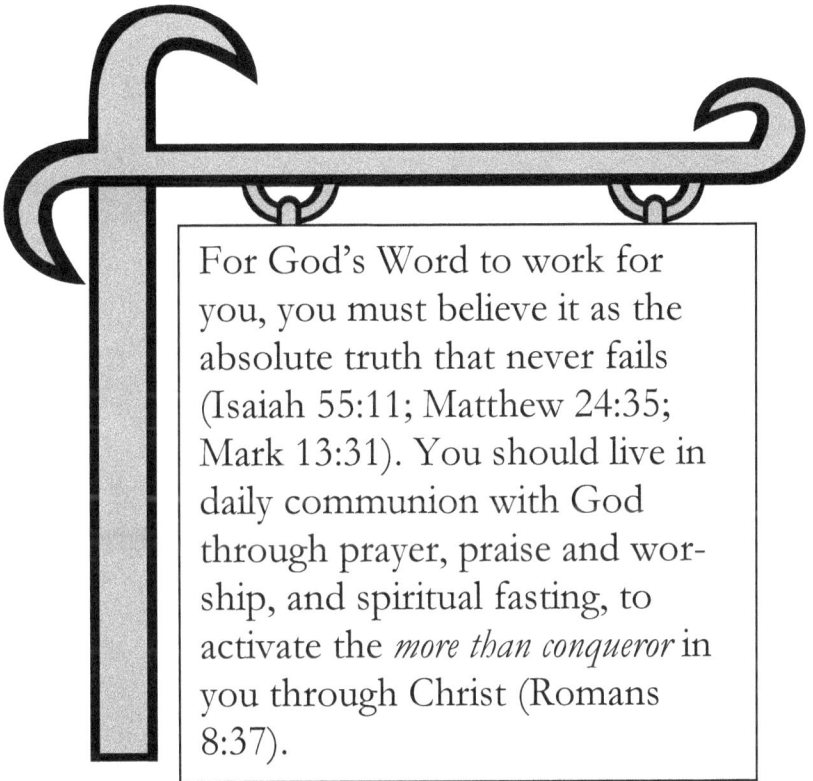

For God's Word to work for you, you must believe it as the absolute truth that never fails (Isaiah 55:11; Matthew 24:35; Mark 13:31). You should live in daily communion with God through prayer, praise and worship, and spiritual fasting, to activate the *more than conqueror* in you through Christ (Romans 8:37).

16

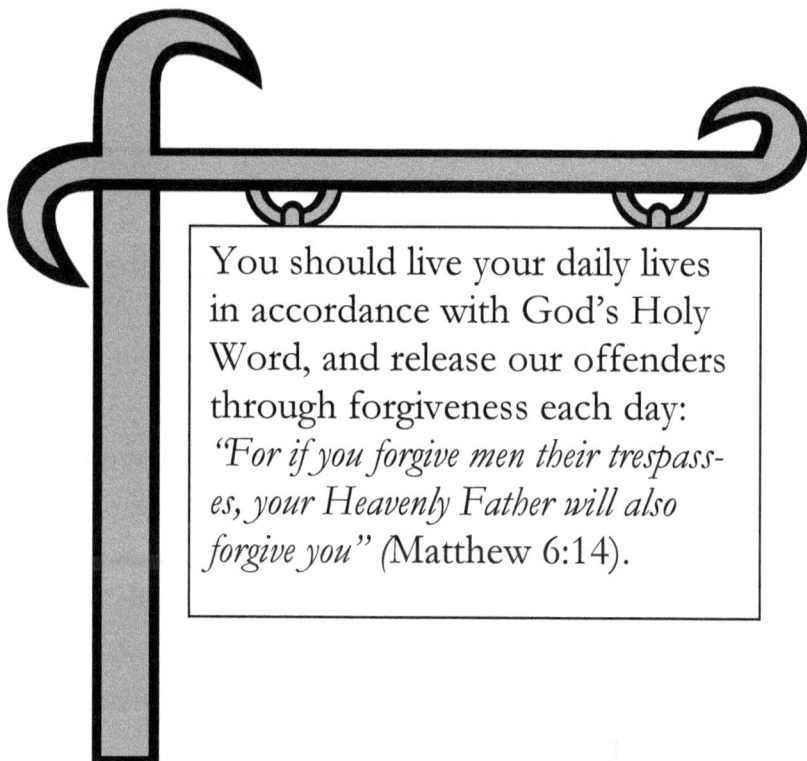

You should live your daily lives in accordance with God's Holy Word, and release our offenders through forgiveness each day: *"For if you forgive men their trespasses, your Heavenly Father will also forgive you"* (Matthew 6:14).

17

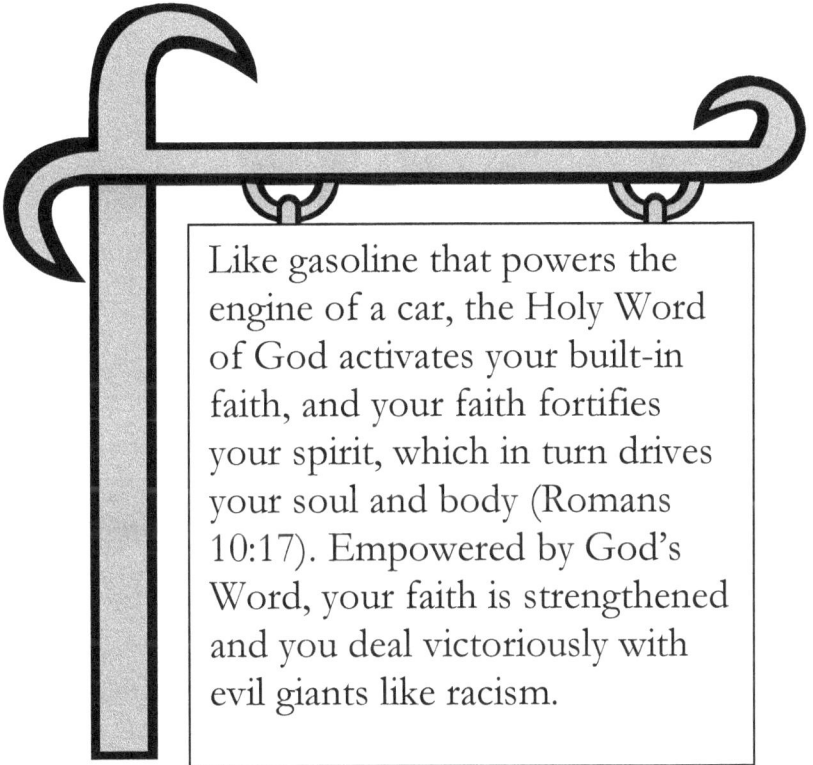

Like gasoline that powers the engine of a car, the Holy Word of God activates your built-in faith, and your faith fortifies your spirit, which in turn drives your soul and body (Romans 10:17). Empowered by God's Word, your faith is strengthened and you deal victoriously with evil giants like racism.

18

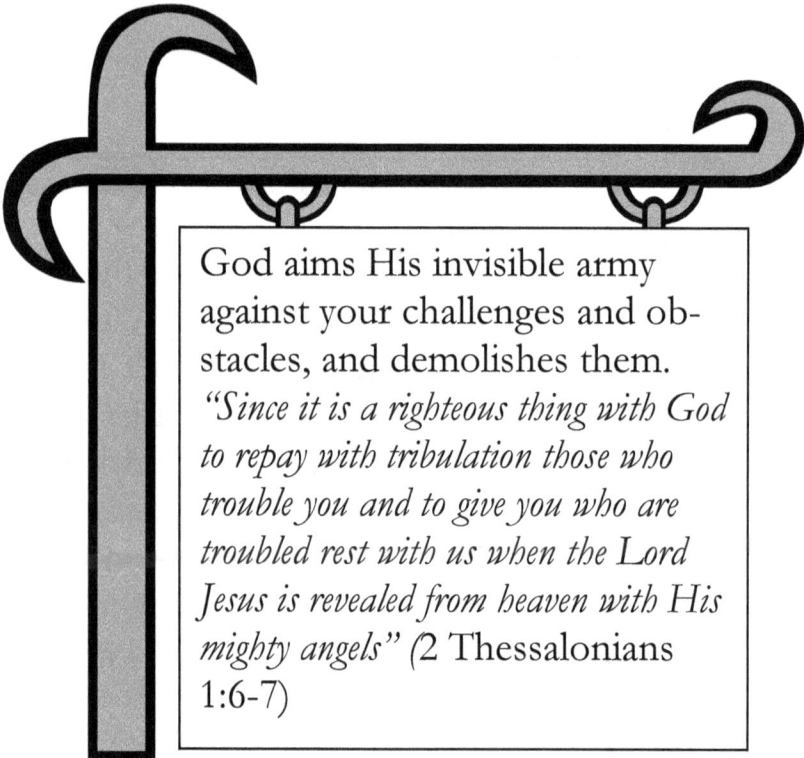

God aims His invisible army against your challenges and obstacles, and demolishes them. *"Since it is a righteous thing with God to repay with tribulation those who trouble you and to give you who are troubled rest with us when the Lord Jesus is revealed from heaven with His mighty angels"* (2 Thessalonians 1:6-7)

19

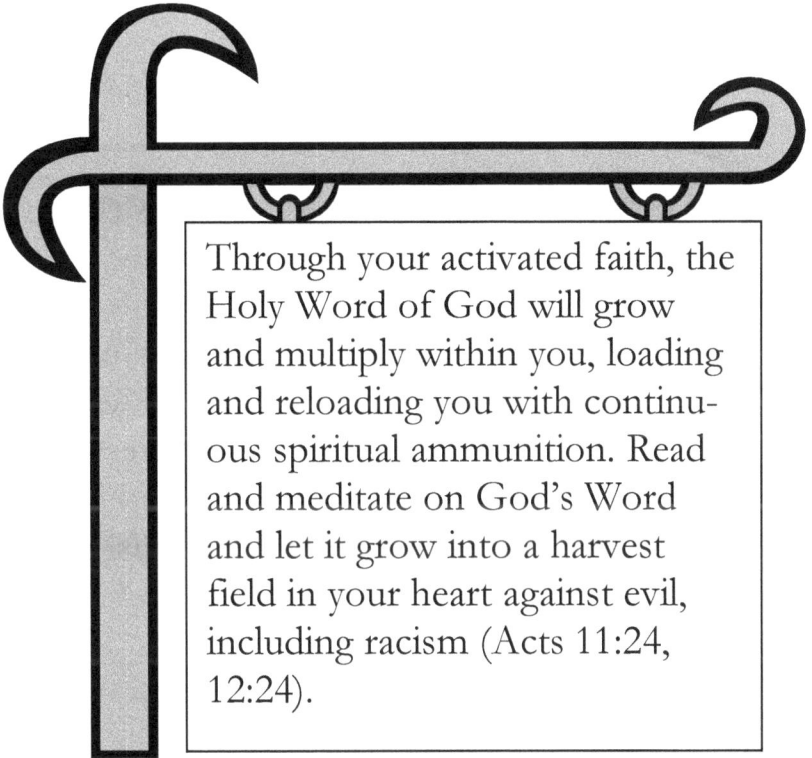

Through your activated faith, the Holy Word of God will grow and multiply within you, loading and reloading you with continuous spiritual ammunition. Read and meditate on God's Word and let it grow into a harvest field in your heart against evil, including racism (Acts 11:24, 12:24).

20

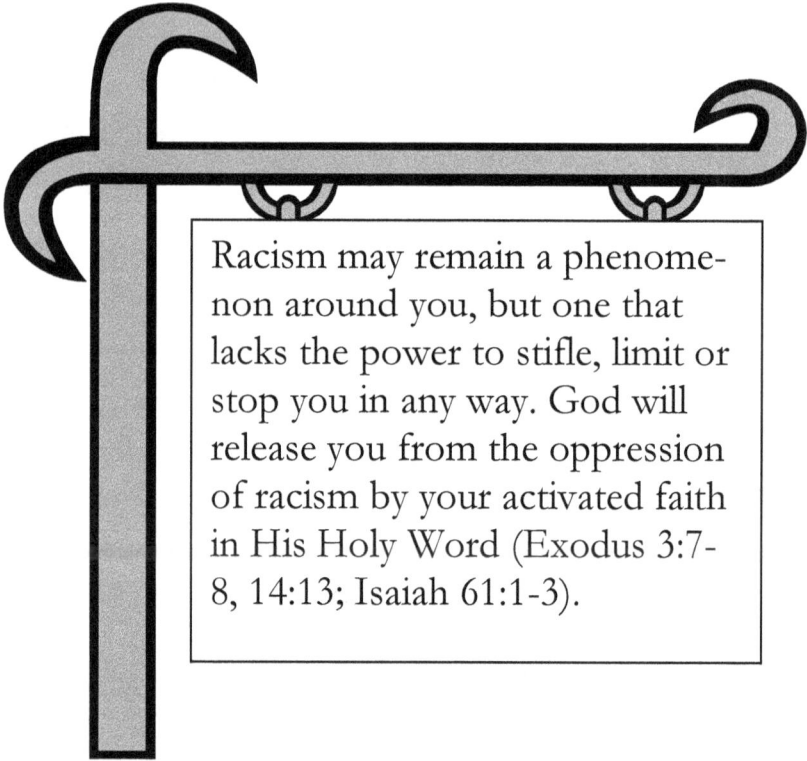

Racism may remain a phenomenon around you, but one that lacks the power to stifle, limit or stop you in any way. God will release you from the oppression of racism by your activated faith in His Holy Word (Exodus 3:7-8, 14:13; Isaiah 61:1-3).

21

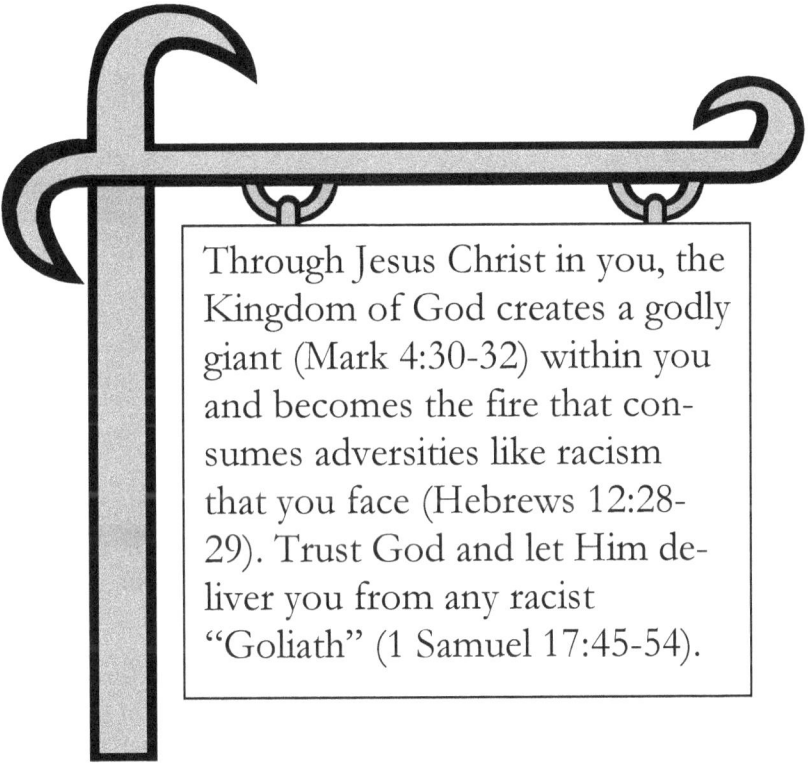

Through Jesus Christ in you, the Kingdom of God creates a godly giant (Mark 4:30-32) within you and becomes the fire that consumes adversities like racism that you face (Hebrews 12:28-29). Trust God and let Him deliver you from any racist "Goliath" (1 Samuel 17:45-54).

22

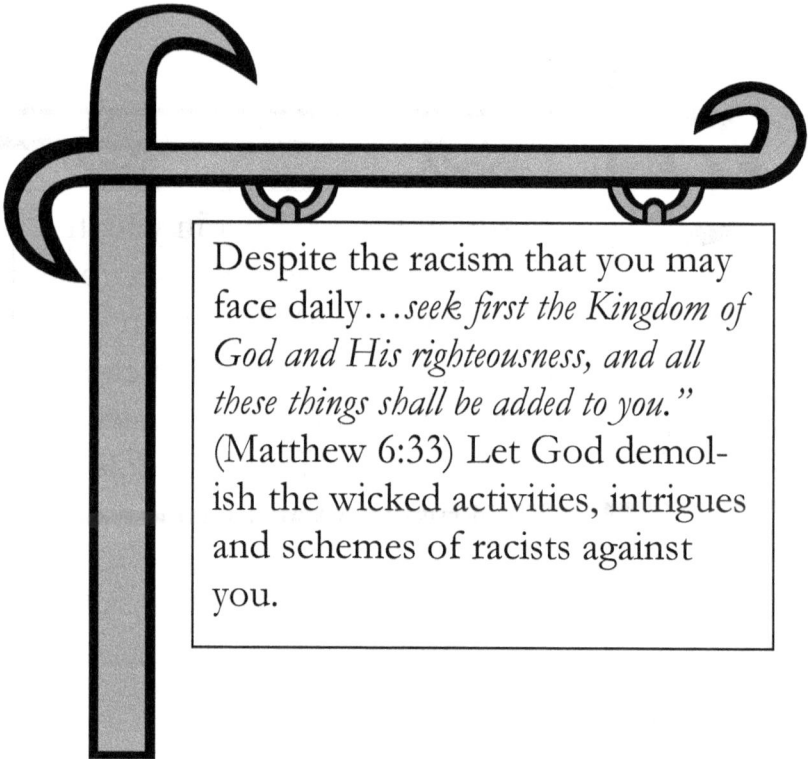

Despite the racism that you may face daily…*seek first the Kingdom of God and His righteousness, and all these things shall be added to you."* (Matthew 6:33) Let God demolish the wicked activities, intrigues and schemes of racists against you.

23

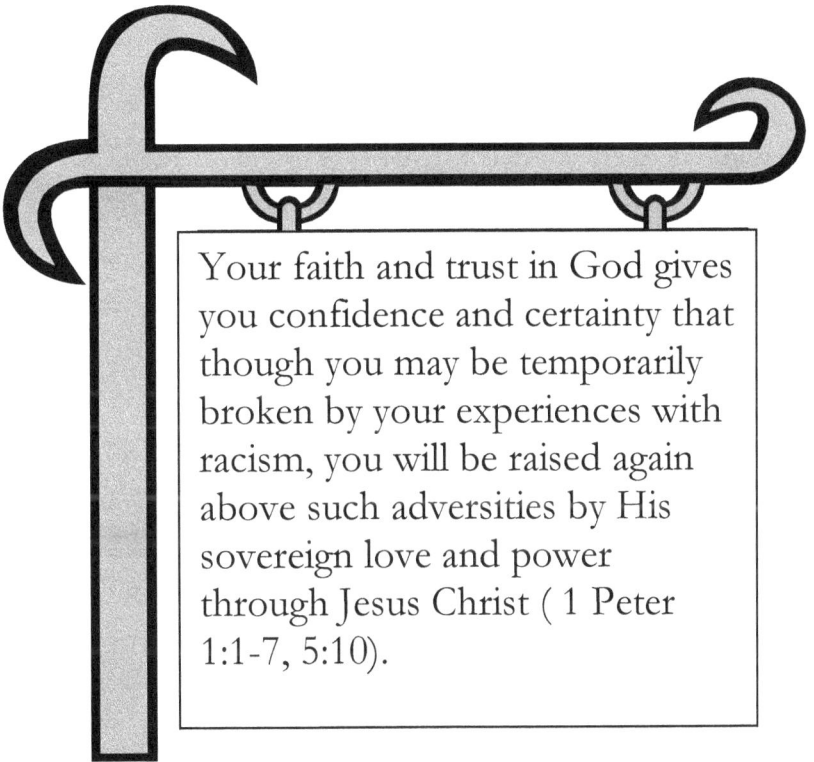

Your faith and trust in God gives you confidence and certainty that though you may be temporarily broken by your experiences with racism, you will be raised again above such adversities by His sovereign love and power through Jesus Christ (1 Peter 1:1-7, 5:10).

24

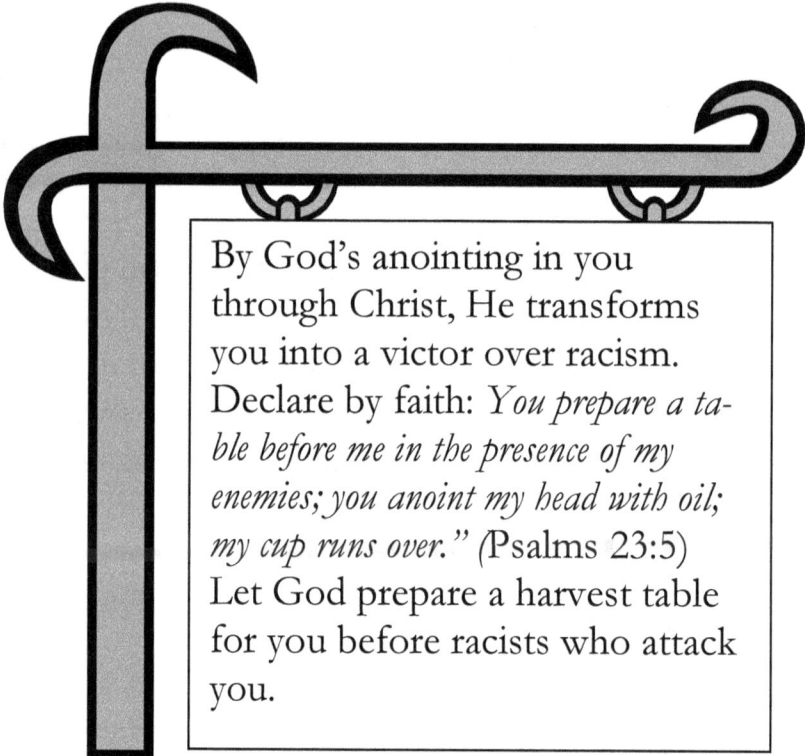

By God's anointing in you through Christ, He transforms you into a victor over racism. Declare by faith: *You prepare a table before me in the presence of my enemies; you anoint my head with oil; my cup runs over."* (Psalms 23:5) Let God prepare a harvest table for you before racists who attack you.

25

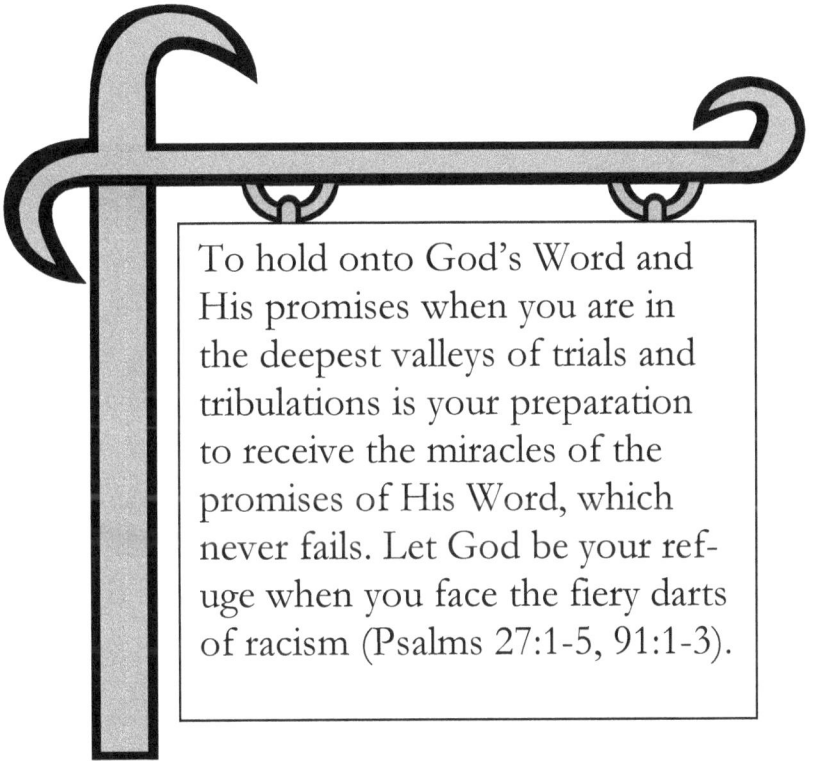

To hold onto God's Word and His promises when you are in the deepest valleys of trials and tribulations is your preparation to receive the miracles of the promises of His Word, which never fails. Let God be your refuge when you face the fiery darts of racism (Psalms 27:1-5, 91:1-3).

26

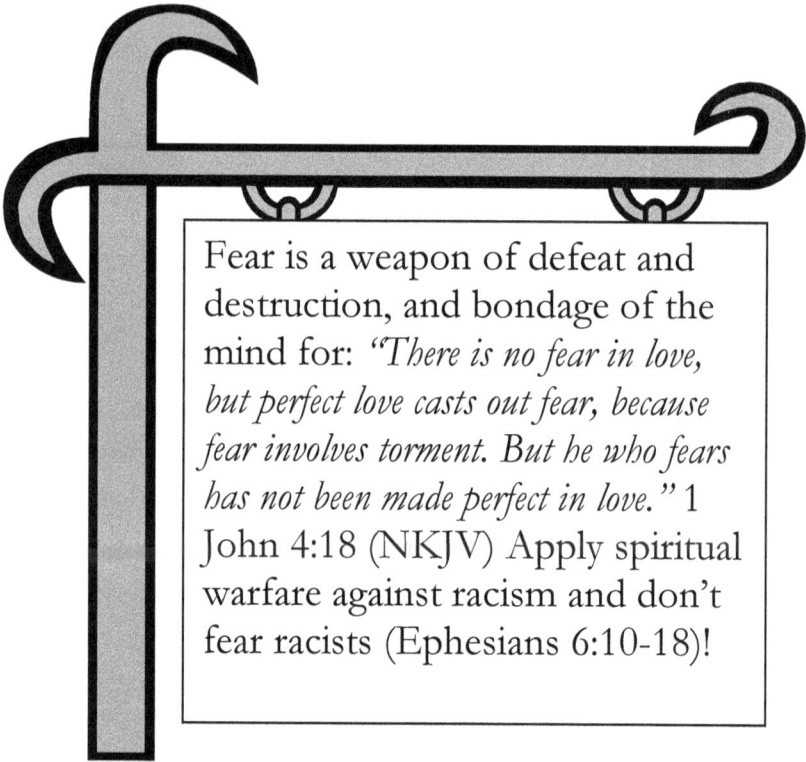

Fear is a weapon of defeat and destruction, and bondage of the mind for: *"There is no fear in love, but perfect love casts out fear, because fear involves torment. But he who fears has not been made perfect in love."* 1 John 4:18 (NKJV) Apply spiritual warfare against racism and don't fear racists (Ephesians 6:10-18)!

27

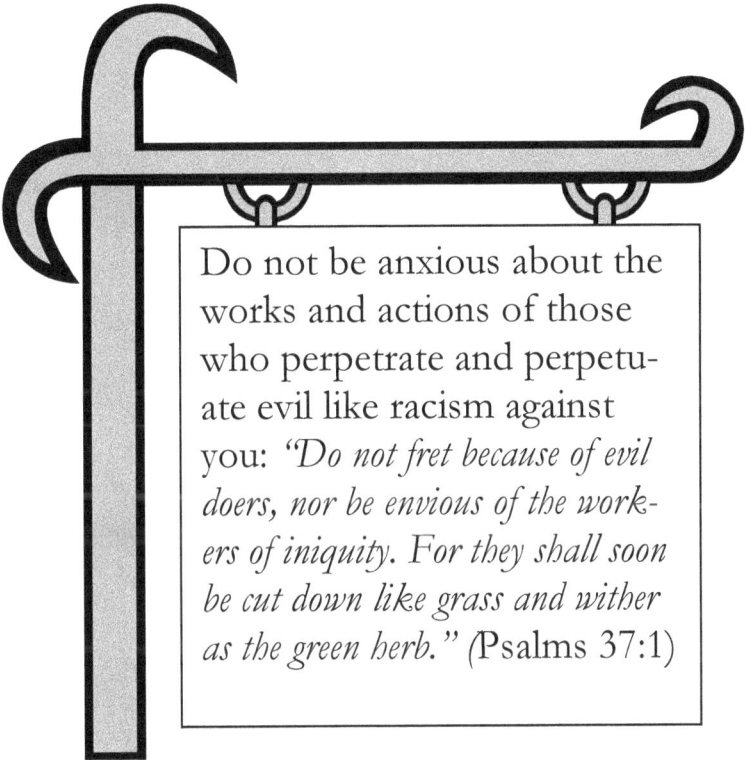

Do not be anxious about the works and actions of those who perpetrate and perpetuate evil like racism against you: *"Do not fret because of evil doers, nor be envious of the workers of iniquity. For they shall soon be cut down like grass and wither as the green herb."* (Psalms 37:1)

28

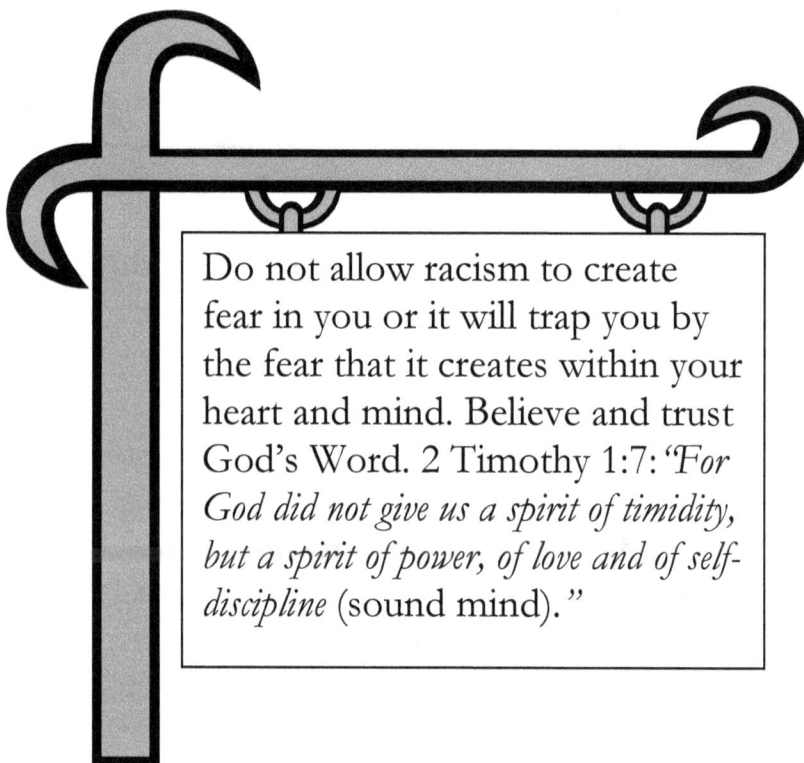

Do not allow racism to create fear in you or it will trap you by the fear that it creates within your heart and mind. Believe and trust God's Word. 2 Timothy 1:7: *"For God did not give us a spirit of timidity, but a spirit of power, of love and of self-discipline* (sound mind)."

29

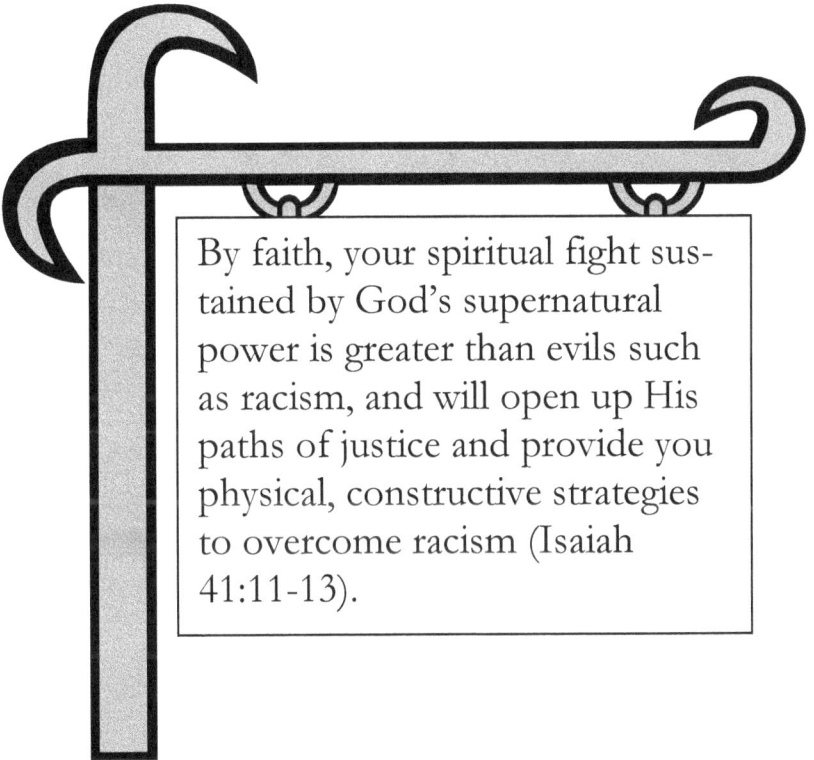

By faith, your spiritual fight sustained by God's supernatural power is greater than evils such as racism, and will open up His paths of justice and provide you physical, constructive strategies to overcome racism (Isaiah 41:11-13).

30

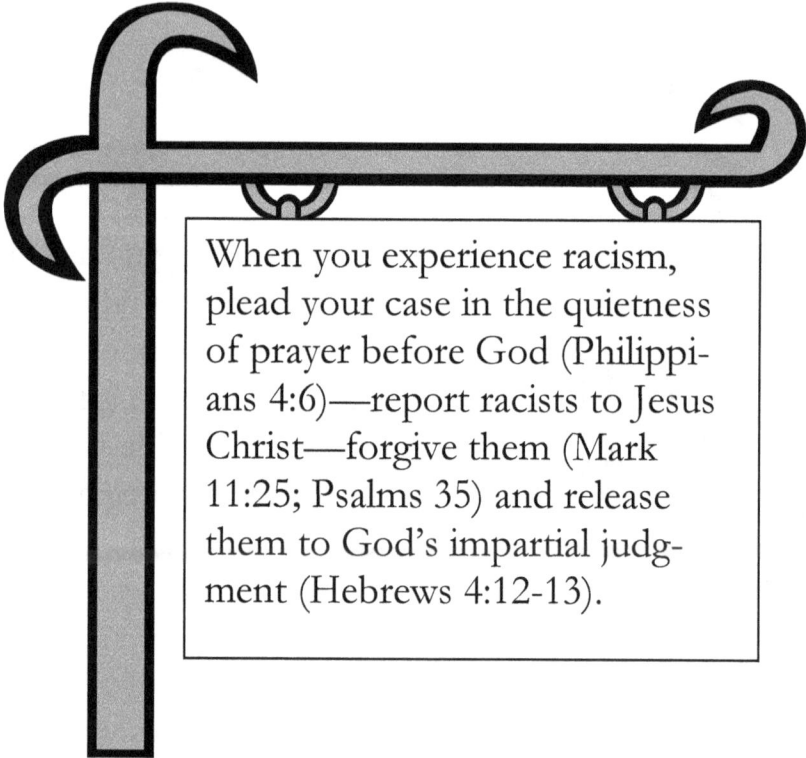

When you experience racism, plead your case in the quietness of prayer before God (Philippians 4:6)—report racists to Jesus Christ—forgive them (Mark 11:25; Psalms 35) and release them to God's impartial judgment (Hebrews 4:12-13).

31

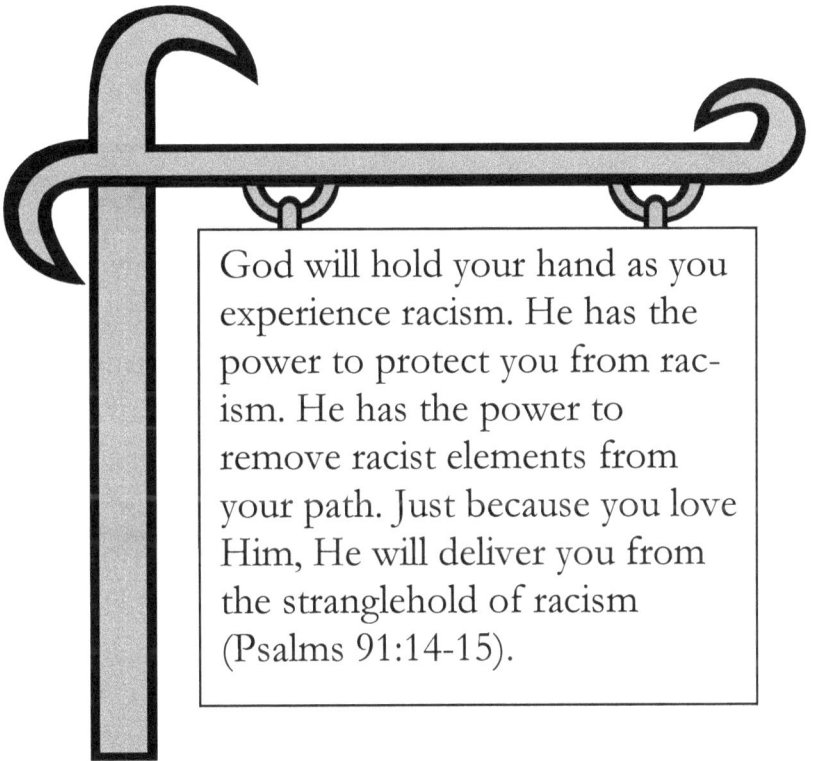

God will hold your hand as you experience racism. He has the power to protect you from racism. He has the power to remove racist elements from your path. Just because you love Him, He will deliver you from the stranglehold of racism (Psalms 91:14-15).

32

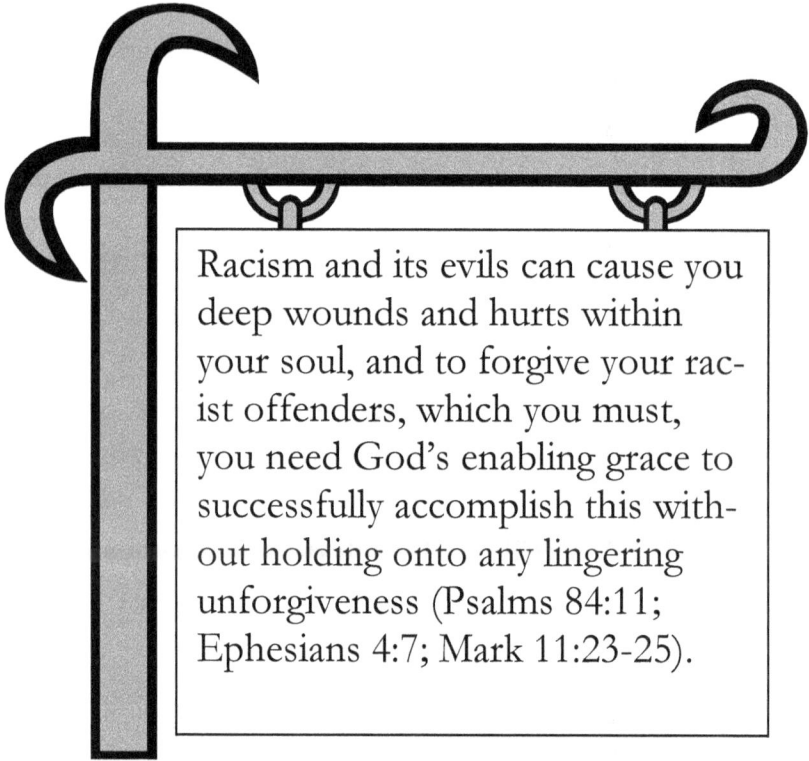

Racism and its evils can cause you deep wounds and hurts within your soul, and to forgive your racist offenders, which you must, you need God's enabling grace to successfully accomplish this without holding onto any lingering unforgiveness (Psalms 84:11; Ephesians 4:7; Mark 11:23-25).

33

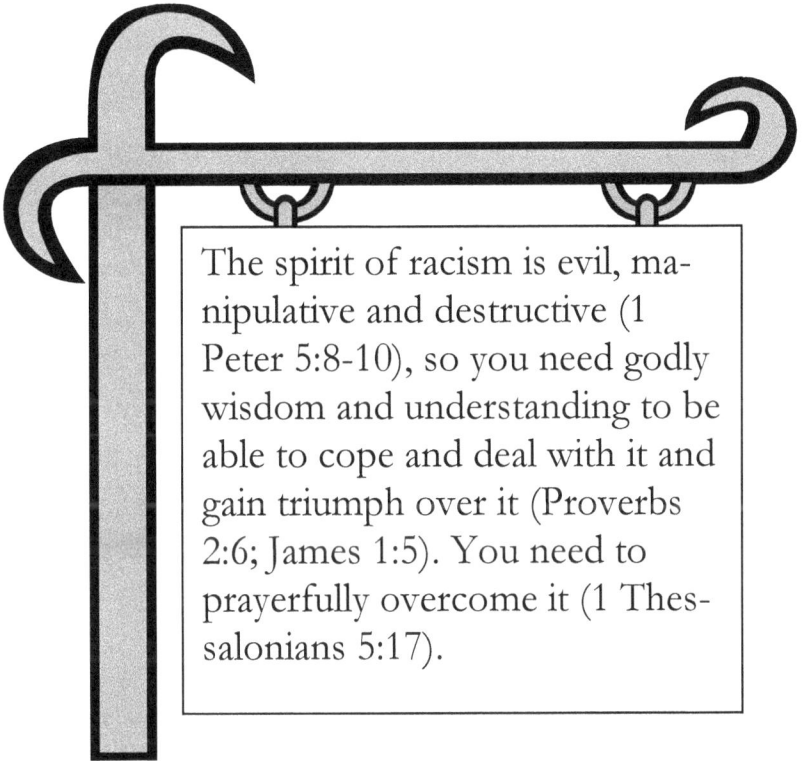

The spirit of racism is evil, manipulative and destructive (1 Peter 5:8-10), so you need godly wisdom and understanding to be able to cope and deal with it and gain triumph over it (Proverbs 2:6; James 1:5). You need to prayerfully overcome it (1 Thessalonians 5:17).

34

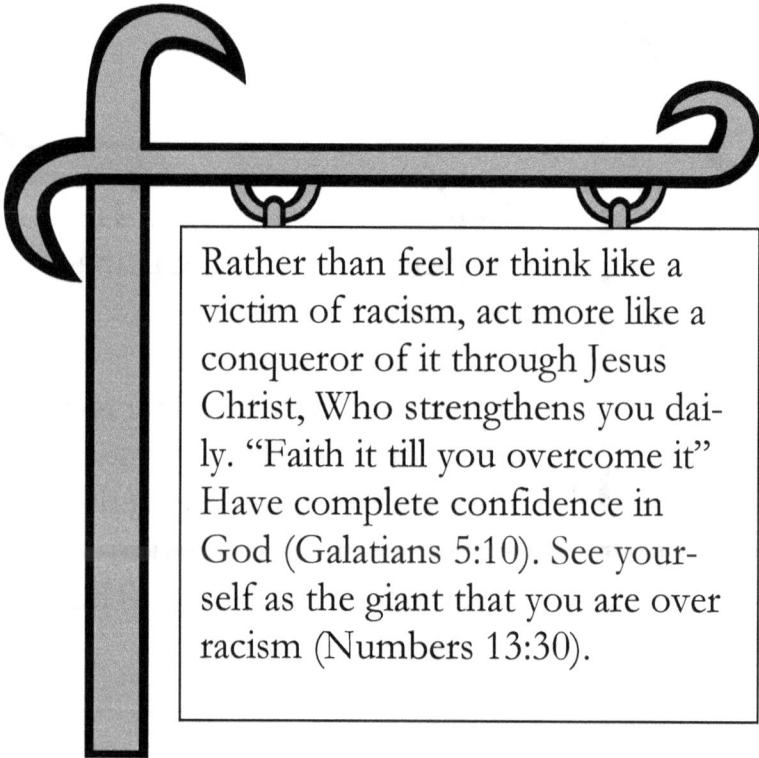

Rather than feel or think like a victim of racism, act more like a conqueror of it through Jesus Christ, Who strengthens you daily. "Faith it till you overcome it" Have complete confidence in God (Galatians 5:10). See yourself as the giant that you are over racism (Numbers 13:30).

35

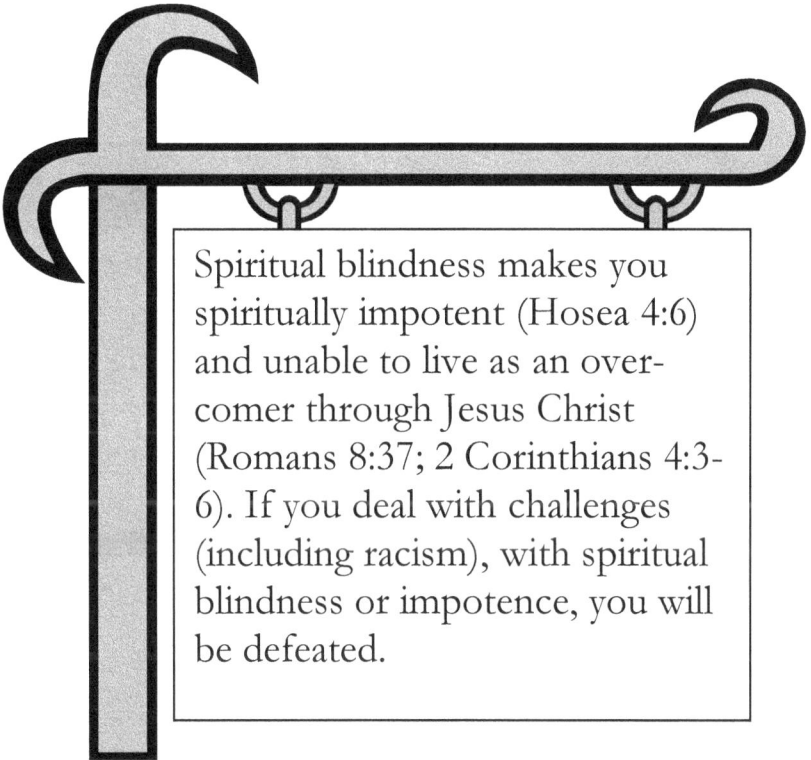

Spiritual blindness makes you spiritually impotent (Hosea 4:6) and unable to live as an overcomer through Jesus Christ (Romans 8:37; 2 Corinthians 4:3-6). If you deal with challenges (including racism), with spiritual blindness or impotence, you will be defeated.

36

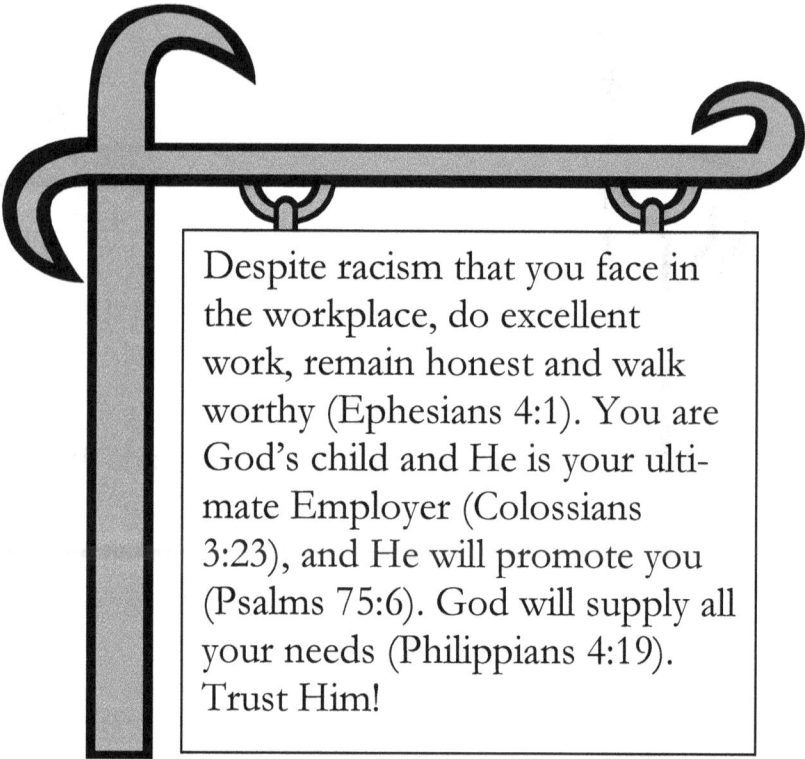

Despite racism that you face in the workplace, do excellent work, remain honest and walk worthy (Ephesians 4:1). You are God's child and He is your ultimate Employer (Colossians 3:23), and He will promote you (Psalms 75:6). God will supply all your needs (Philippians 4:19). Trust Him!

37

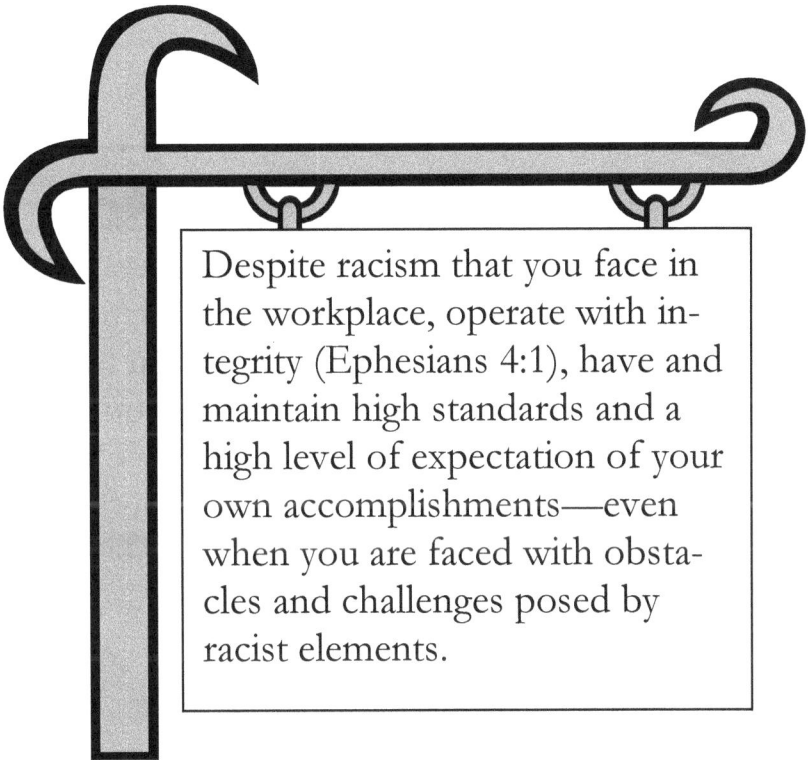

Despite racism that you face in the workplace, operate with integrity (Ephesians 4:1), have and maintain high standards and a high level of expectation of your own accomplishments—even when you are faced with obstacles and challenges posed by racist elements.

38

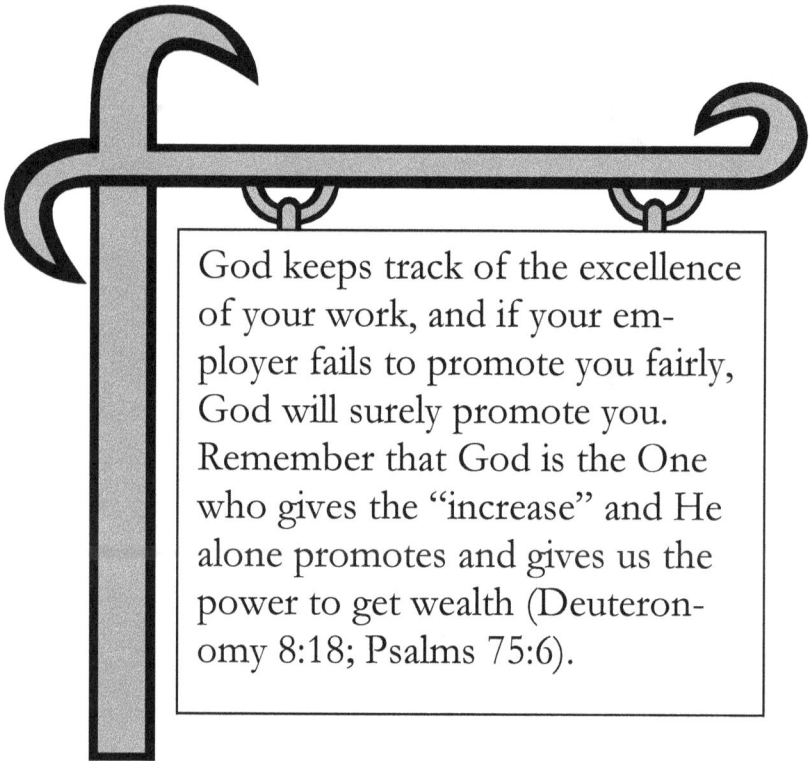

God keeps track of the excellence of your work, and if your employer fails to promote you fairly, God will surely promote you. Remember that God is the One who gives the "increase" and He alone promotes and gives us the power to get wealth (Deuteronomy 8:18; Psalms 75:6).

39

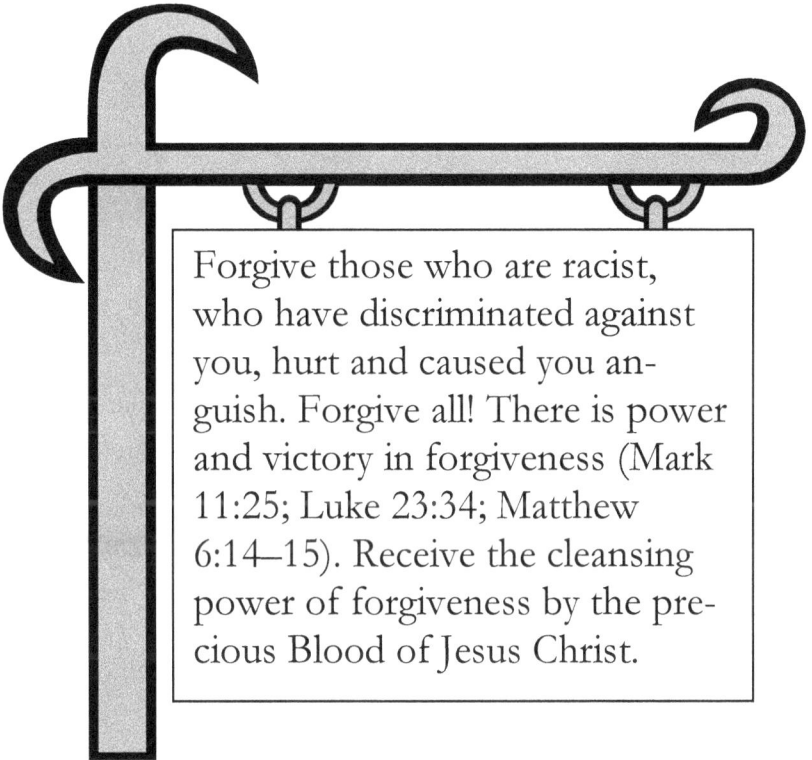

Forgive those who are racist, who have discriminated against you, hurt and caused you anguish. Forgive all! There is power and victory in forgiveness (Mark 11:25; Luke 23:34; Matthew 6:14–15). Receive the cleansing power of forgiveness by the precious Blood of Jesus Christ.

40

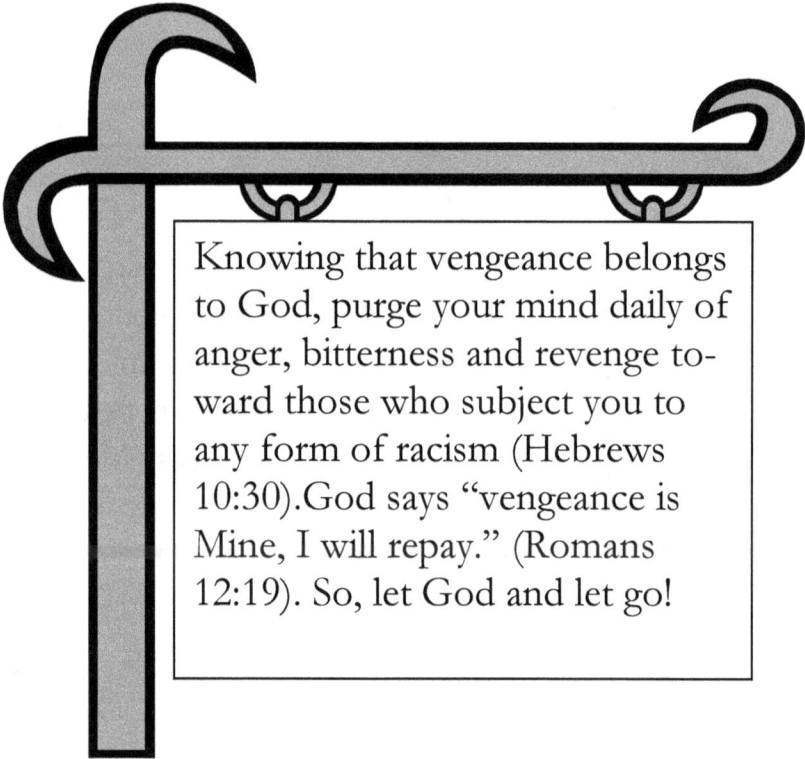

Knowing that vengeance belongs to God, purge your mind daily of anger, bitterness and revenge toward those who subject you to any form of racism (Hebrews 10:30). God says "vengeance is Mine, I will repay." (Romans 12:19). So, let God and let go!

41

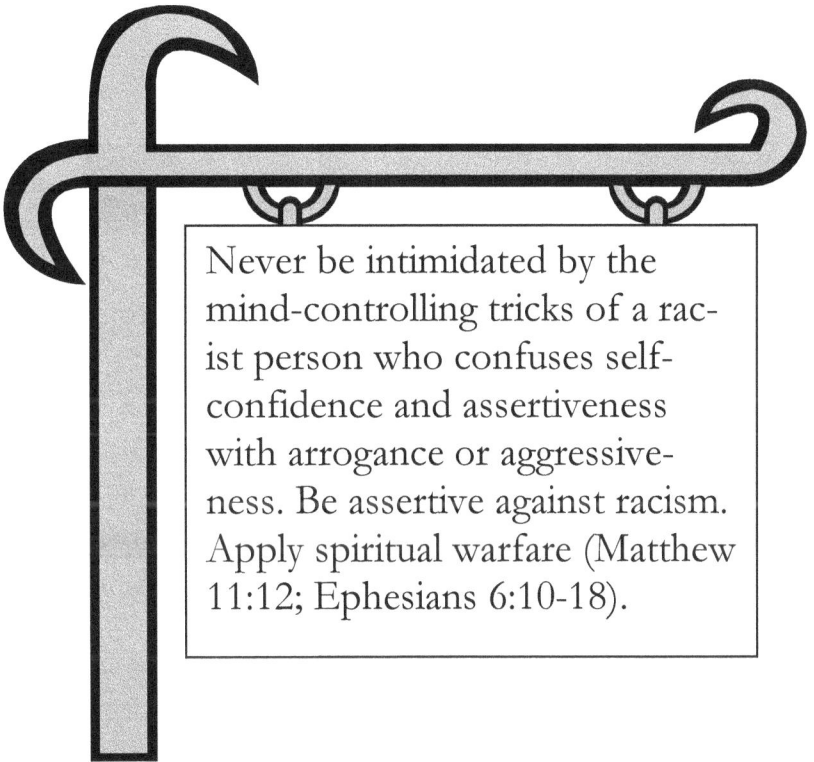

Never be intimidated by the mind-controlling tricks of a racist person who confuses self-confidence and assertiveness with arrogance or aggressiveness. Be assertive against racism. Apply spiritual warfare (Matthew 11:12; Ephesians 6:10-18).

42

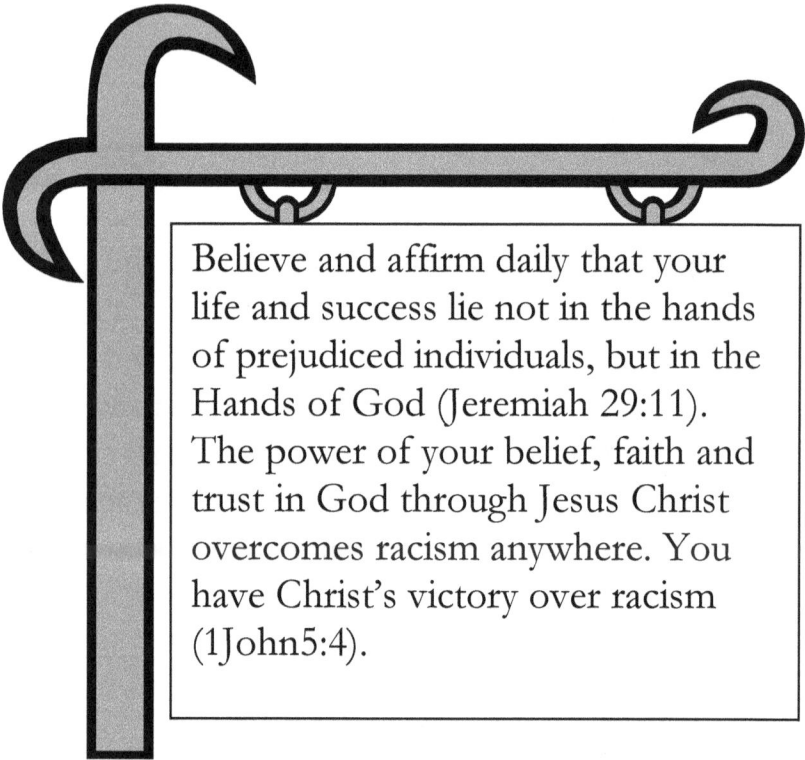

Believe and affirm daily that your life and success lie not in the hands of prejudiced individuals, but in the Hands of God (Jeremiah 29:11). The power of your belief, faith and trust in God through Jesus Christ overcomes racism anywhere. You have Christ's victory over racism (1John5:4).

43

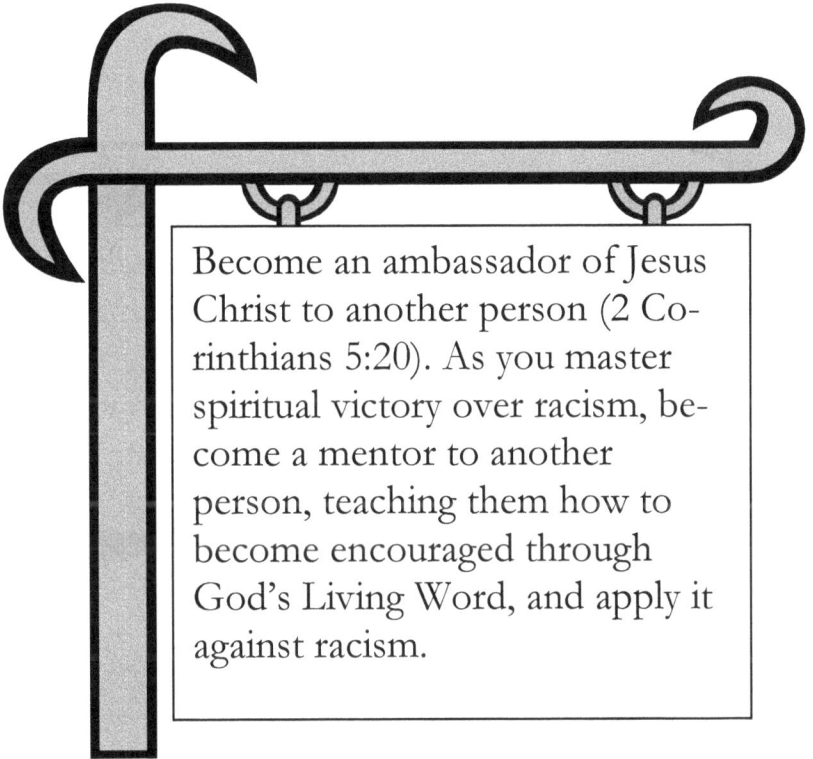

Become an ambassador of Jesus Christ to another person (2 Corinthians 5:20). As you master spiritual victory over racism, become a mentor to another person, teaching them how to become encouraged through God's Living Word, and apply it against racism.

44

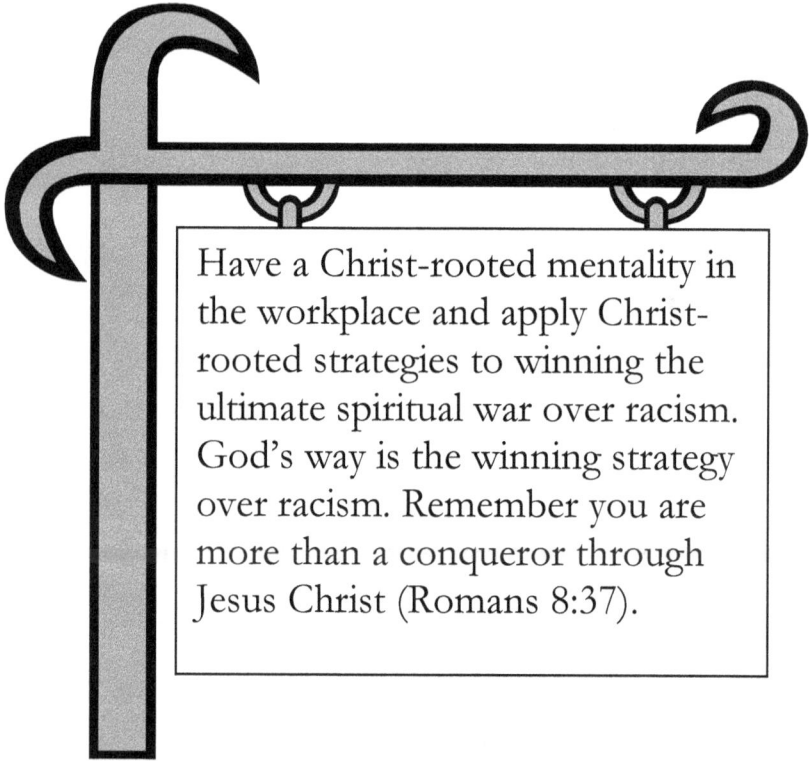

Have a Christ-rooted mentality in the workplace and apply Christ-rooted strategies to winning the ultimate spiritual war over racism. God's way is the winning strategy over racism. Remember you are more than a conqueror through Jesus Christ (Romans 8:37).

45

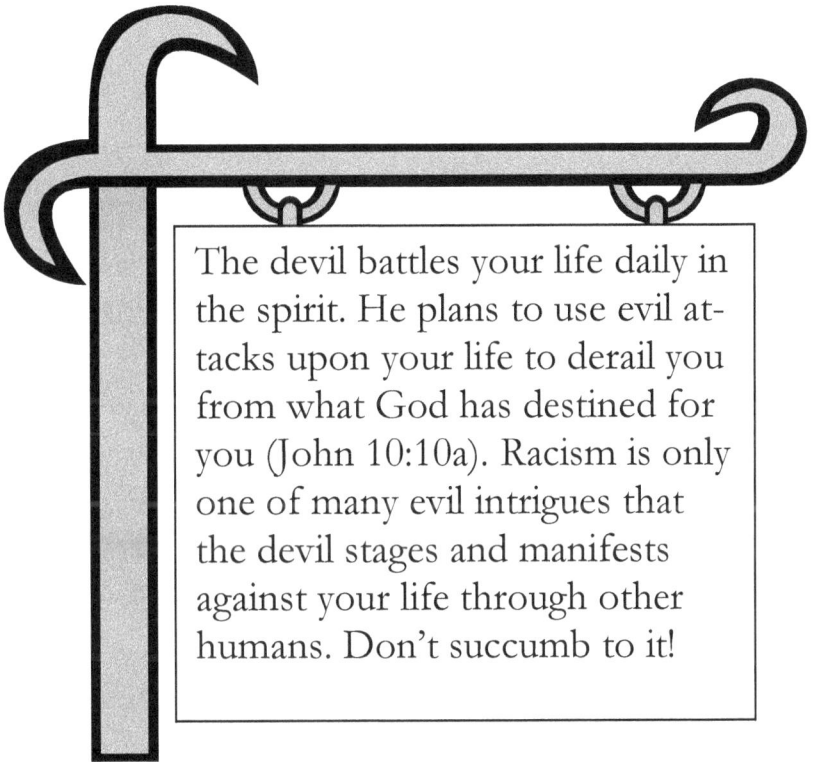

The devil battles your life daily in the spirit. He plans to use evil attacks upon your life to derail you from what God has destined for you (John 10:10a). Racism is only one of many evil intrigues that the devil stages and manifests against your life through other humans. Don't succumb to it!

46

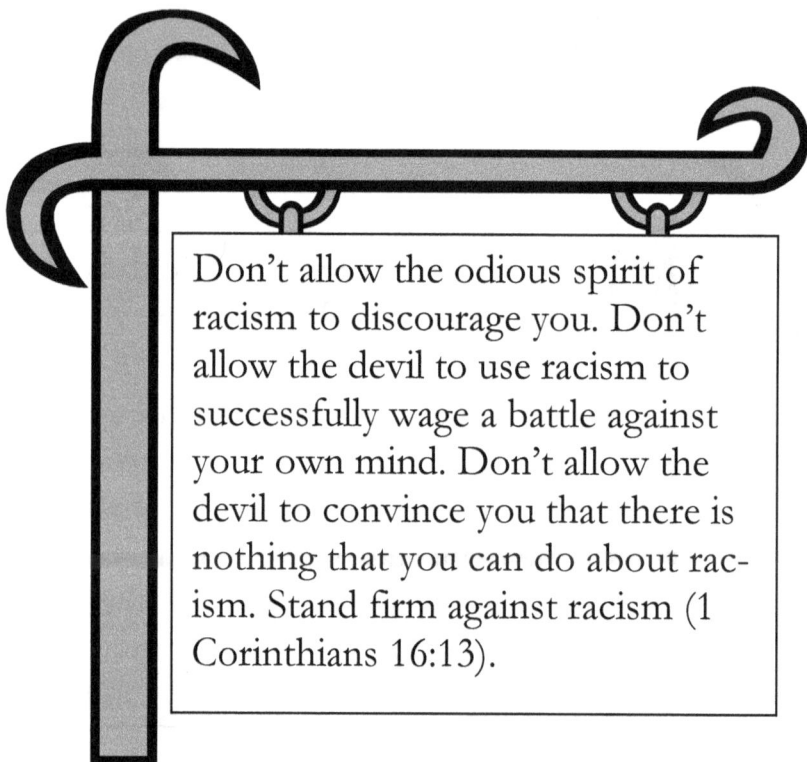

Don't allow the odious spirit of racism to discourage you. Don't allow the devil to use racism to successfully wage a battle against your own mind. Don't allow the devil to convince you that there is nothing that you can do about racism. Stand firm against racism (1 Corinthians 16:13).

47

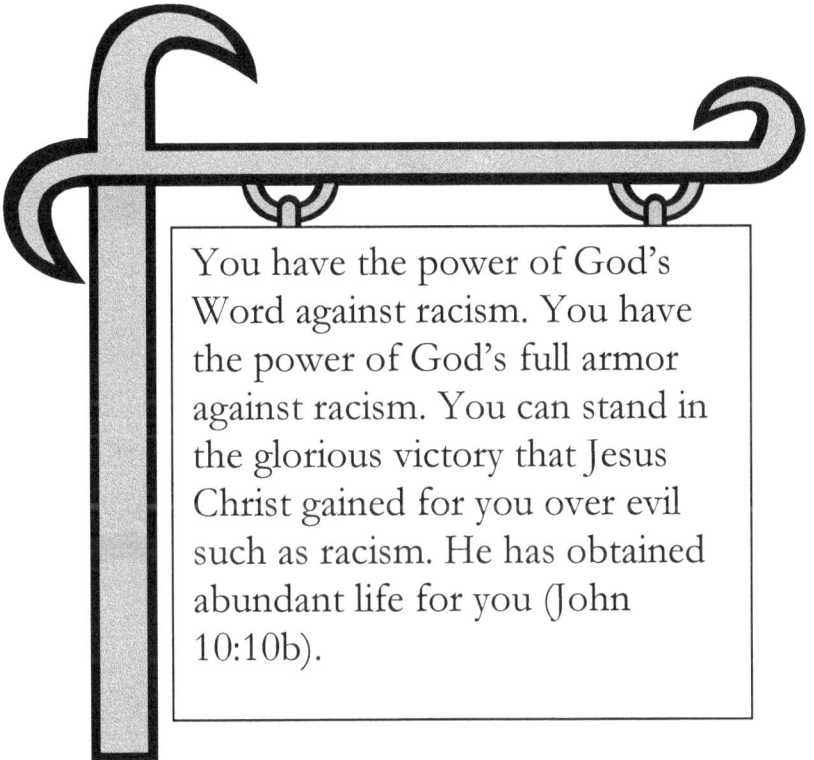

You have the power of God's Word against racism. You have the power of God's full armor against racism. You can stand in the glorious victory that Jesus Christ gained for you over evil such as racism. He has obtained abundant life for you (John 10:10b).

48

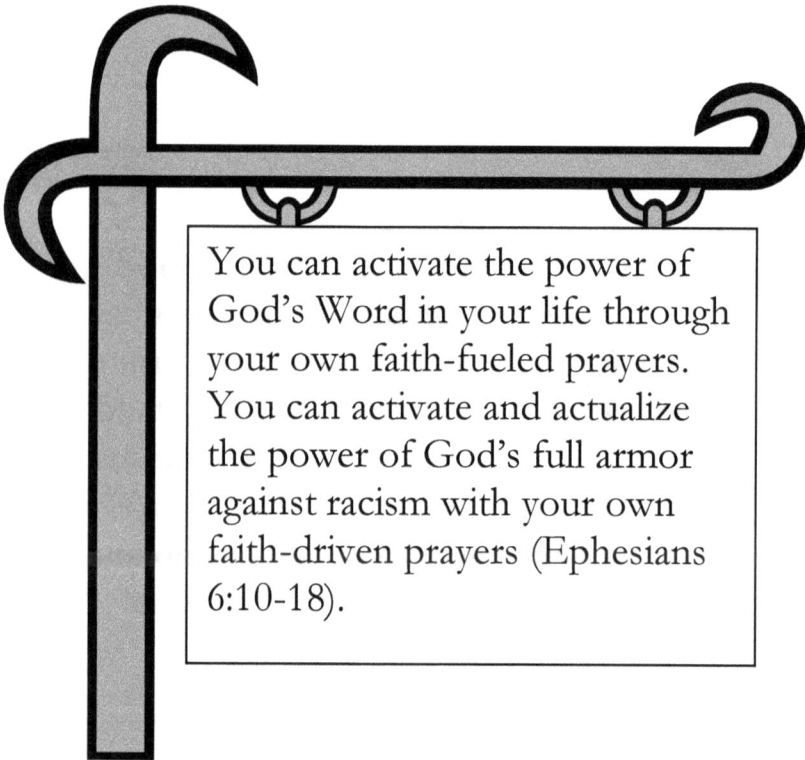

You can activate the power of God's Word in your life through your own faith-fueled prayers. You can activate and actualize the power of God's full armor against racism with your own faith-driven prayers (Ephesians 6:10-18).

49

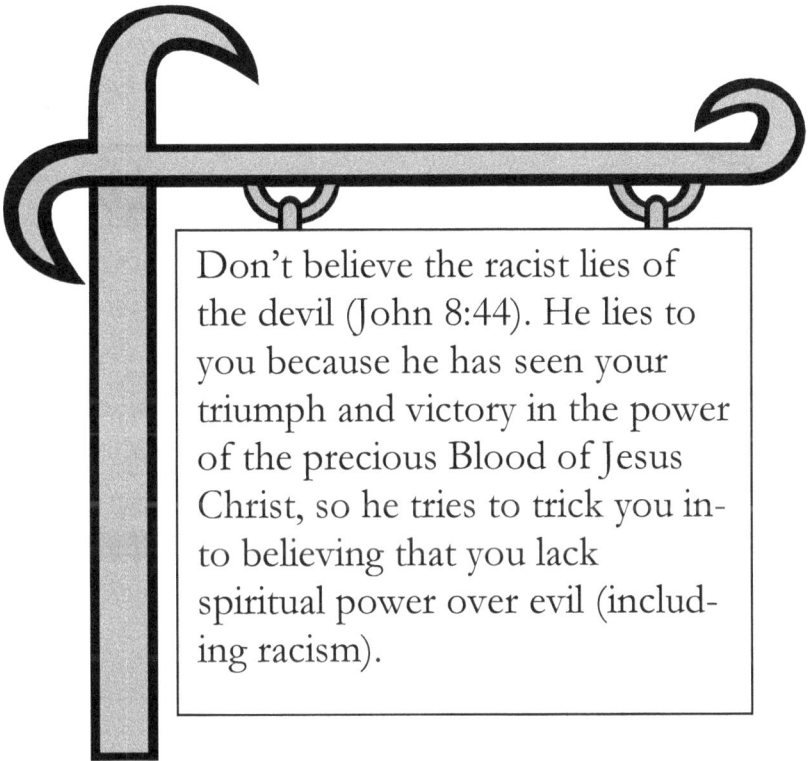

Don't believe the racist lies of the devil (John 8:44). He lies to you because he has seen your triumph and victory in the power of the precious Blood of Jesus Christ, so he tries to trick you into believing that you lack spiritual power over evil (including racism).

50

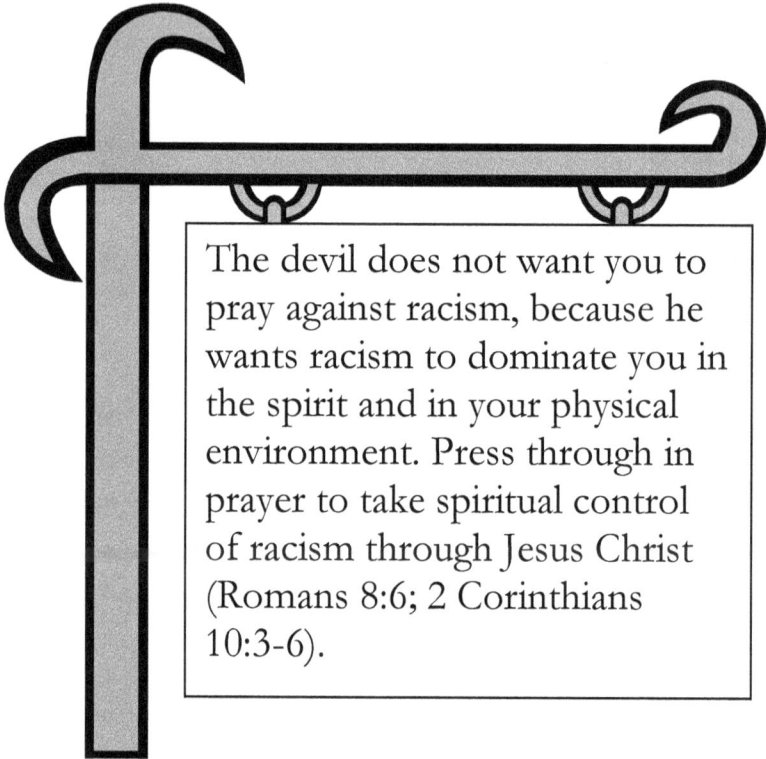

The devil does not want you to pray against racism, because he wants racism to dominate you in the spirit and in your physical environment. Press through in prayer to take spiritual control of racism through Jesus Christ (Romans 8:6; 2 Corinthians 10:3-6).

51

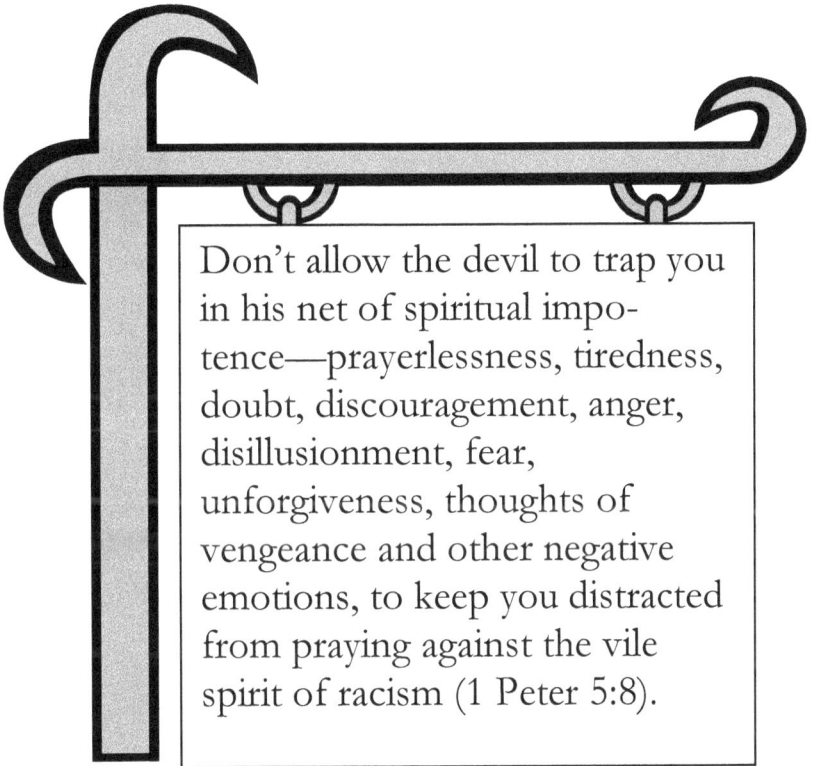

Don't allow the devil to trap you in his net of spiritual impotence—prayerlessness, tiredness, doubt, discouragement, anger, disillusionment, fear, unforgiveness, thoughts of vengeance and other negative emotions, to keep you distracted from praying against the vile spirit of racism (1 Peter 5:8).

52

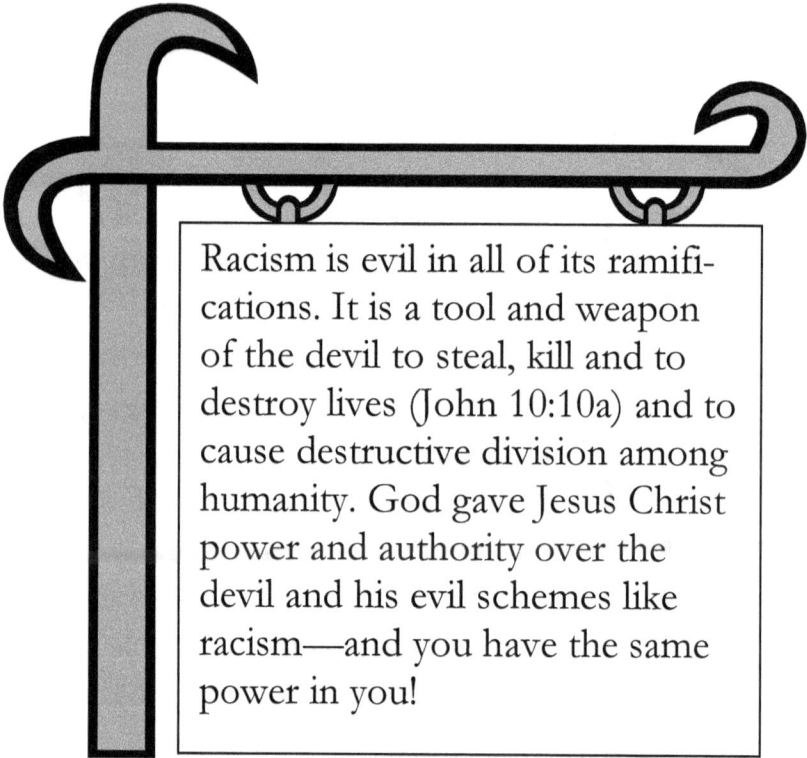

Racism is evil in all of its ramifications. It is a tool and weapon of the devil to steal, kill and to destroy lives (John 10:10a) and to cause destructive division among humanity. God gave Jesus Christ power and authority over the devil and his evil schemes like racism—and you have the same power in you!

53

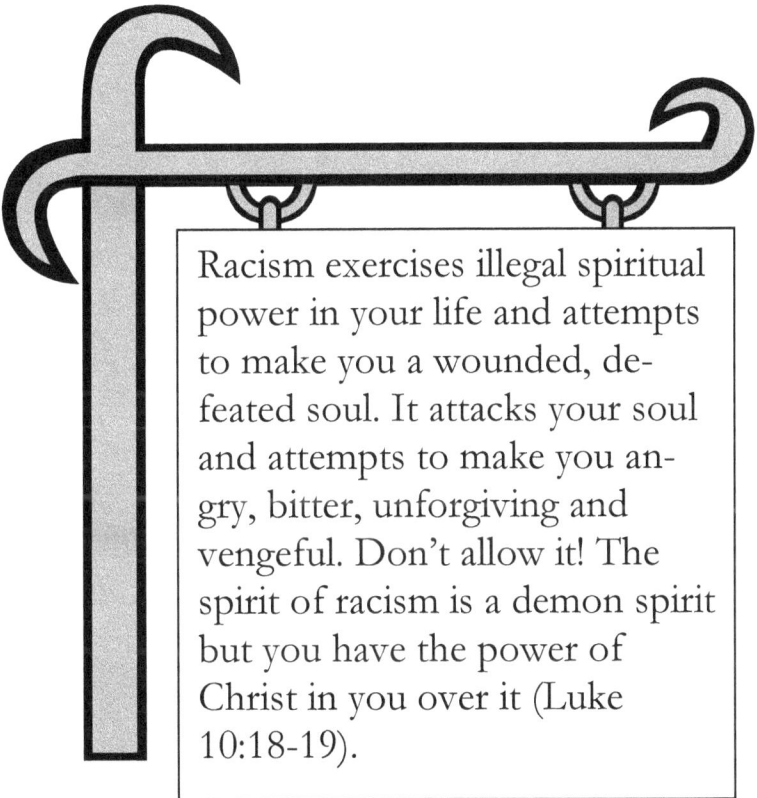

Racism exercises illegal spiritual power in your life and attempts to make you a wounded, defeated soul. It attacks your soul and attempts to make you angry, bitter, unforgiving and vengeful. Don't allow it! The spirit of racism is a demon spirit but you have the power of Christ in you over it (Luke 10:18-19).

54

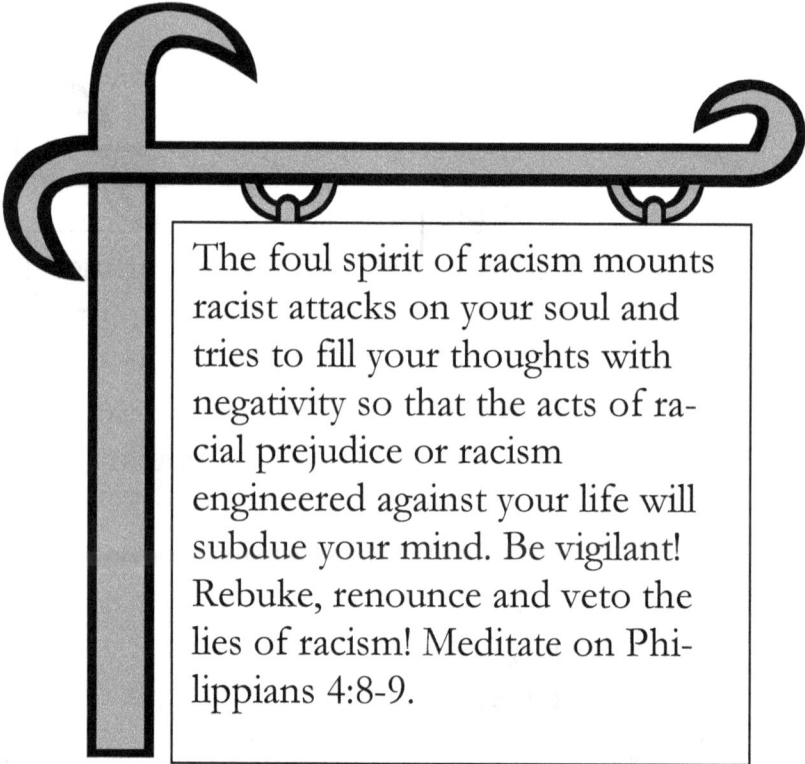

The foul spirit of racism mounts racist attacks on your soul and tries to fill your thoughts with negativity so that the acts of racial prejudice or racism engineered against your life will subdue your mind. Be vigilant! Rebuke, renounce and veto the lies of racism! Meditate on Philippians 4:8-9.

55

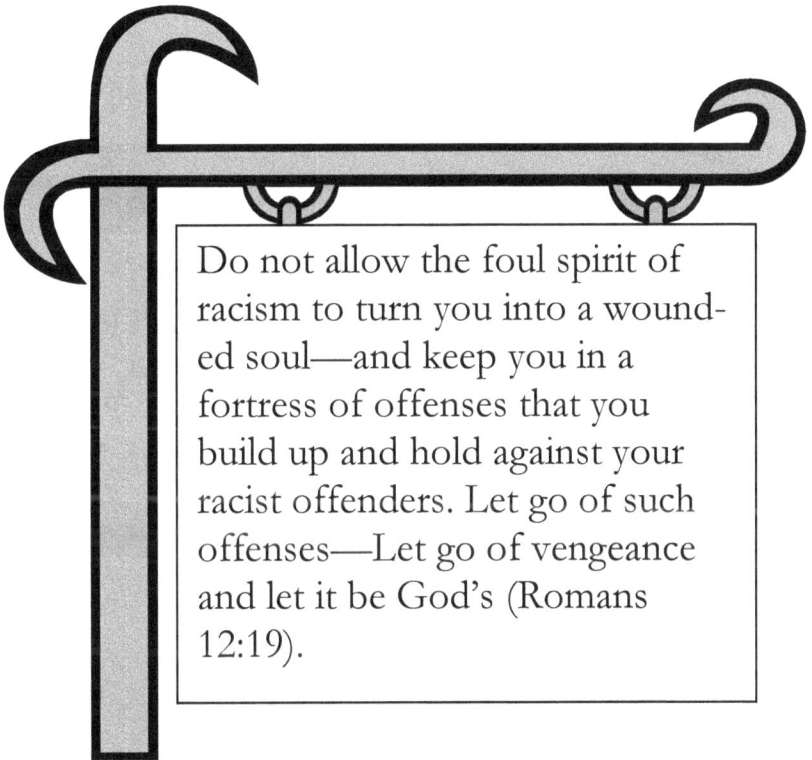

Do not allow the foul spirit of racism to turn you into a wounded soul—and keep you in a fortress of offenses that you build up and hold against your racist offenders. Let go of such offenses—Let go of vengeance and let it be God's (Romans 12:19).

56

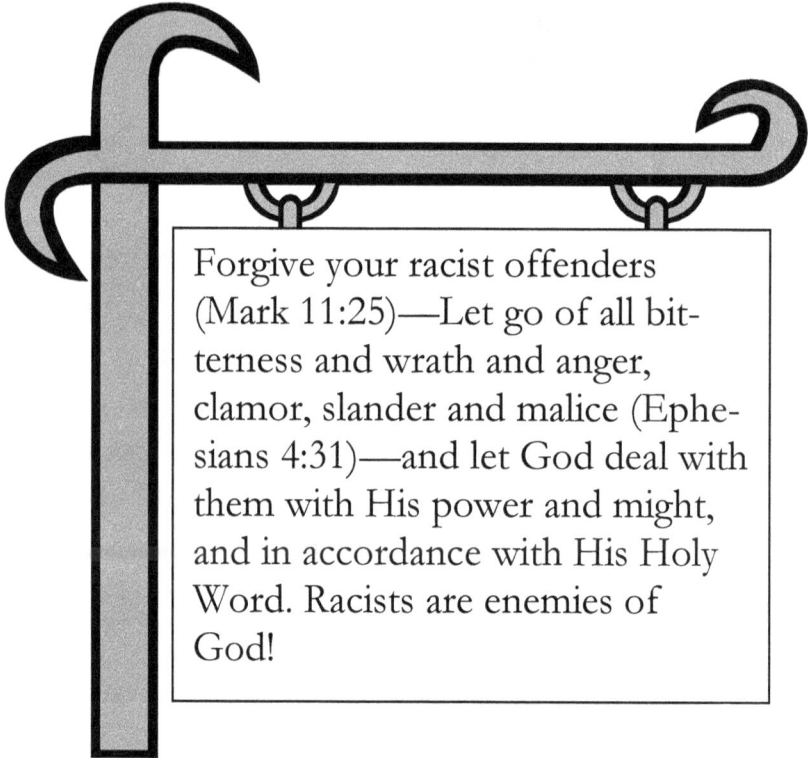

Forgive your racist offenders (Mark 11:25)—Let go of all bitterness and wrath and anger, clamor, slander and malice (Ephesians 4:31)—and let God deal with them with His power and might, and in accordance with His Holy Word. Racists are enemies of God!

57

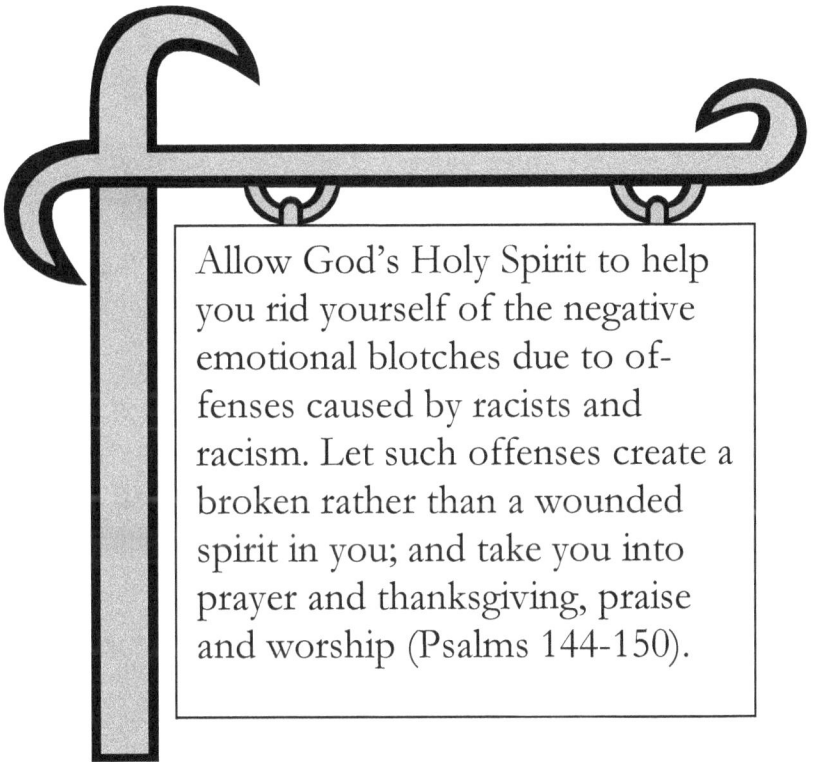

Allow God's Holy Spirit to help you rid yourself of the negative emotional blotches due to offenses caused by racists and racism. Let such offenses create a broken rather than a wounded spirit in you; and take you into prayer and thanksgiving, praise and worship (Psalms 144-150).

58

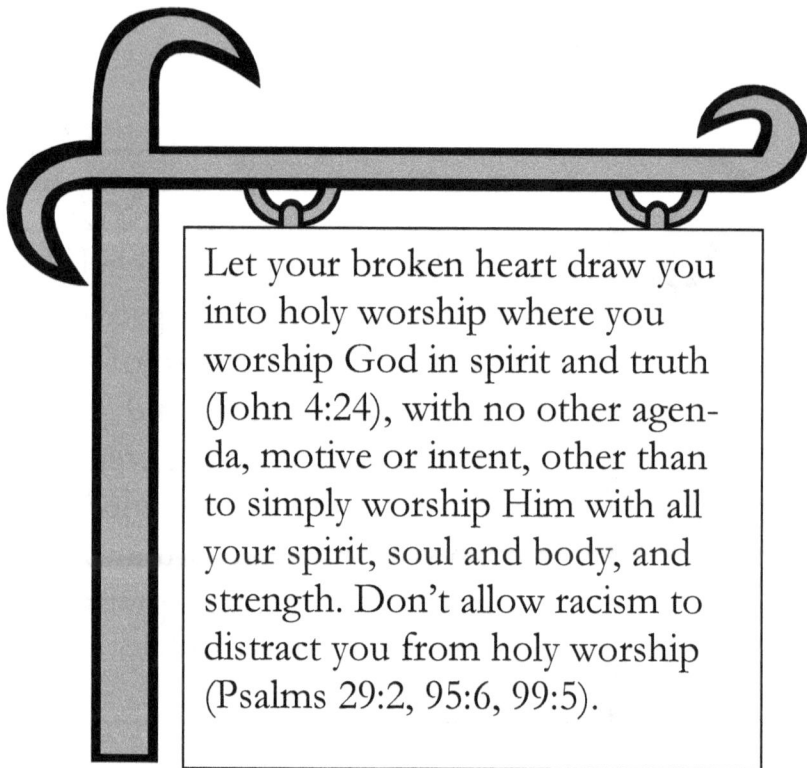

Let your broken heart draw you into holy worship where you worship God in spirit and truth (John 4:24), with no other agenda, motive or intent, other than to simply worship Him with all your spirit, soul and body, and strength. Don't allow racism to distract you from holy worship (Psalms 29:2, 95:6, 99:5).

59

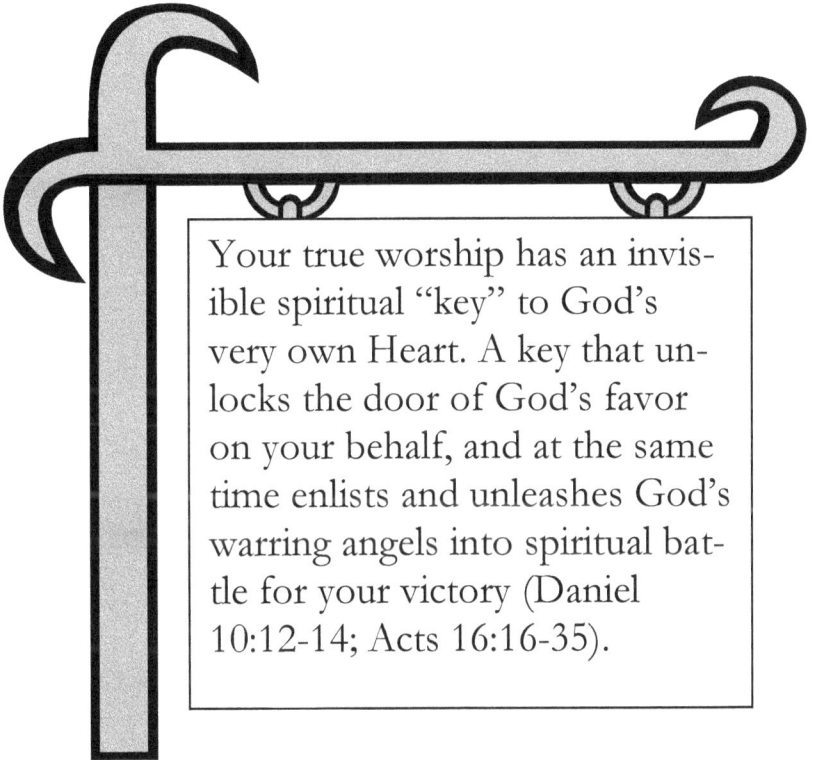

Your true worship has an invisible spiritual "key" to God's very own Heart. A key that unlocks the door of God's favor on your behalf, and at the same time enlists and unleashes God's warring angels into spiritual battle for your victory (Daniel 10:12-14; Acts 16:16-35).

60

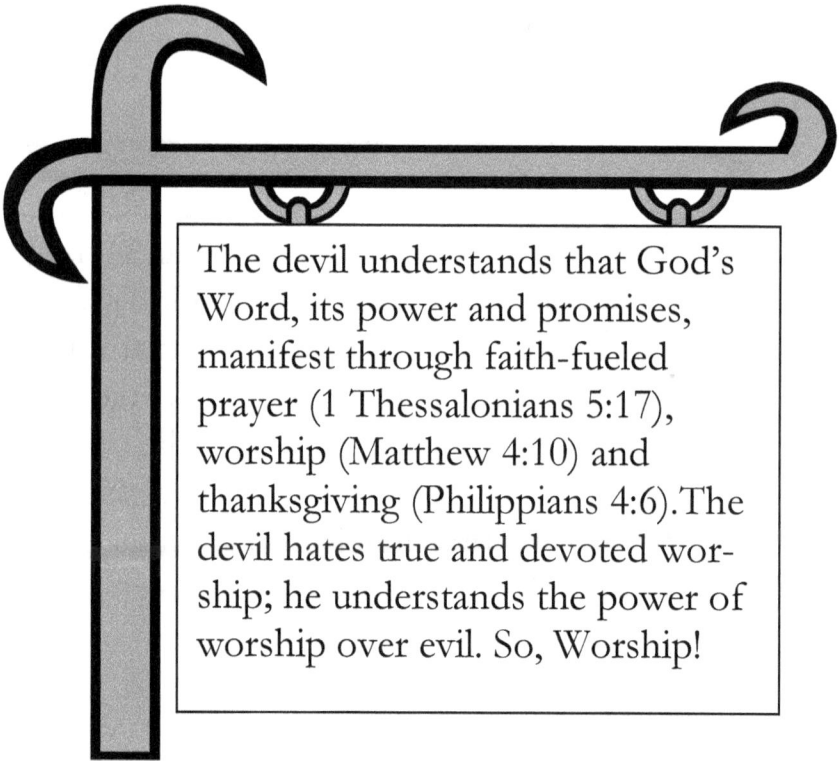

The devil understands that God's Word, its power and promises, manifest through faith-fueled prayer (1 Thessalonians 5:17), worship (Matthew 4:10) and thanksgiving (Philippians 4:6). The devil hates true and devoted worship; he understands the power of worship over evil. So, Worship!

61

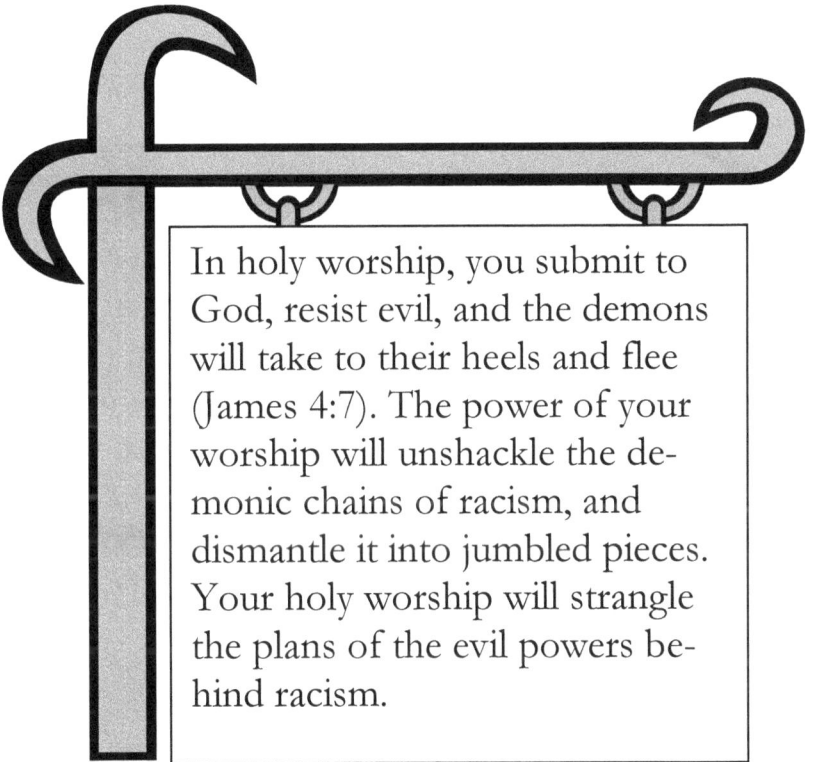

In holy worship, you submit to God, resist evil, and the demons will take to their heels and flee (James 4:7). The power of your worship will unshackle the demonic chains of racism, and dismantle it into jumbled pieces. Your holy worship will strangle the plans of the evil powers behind racism.

62

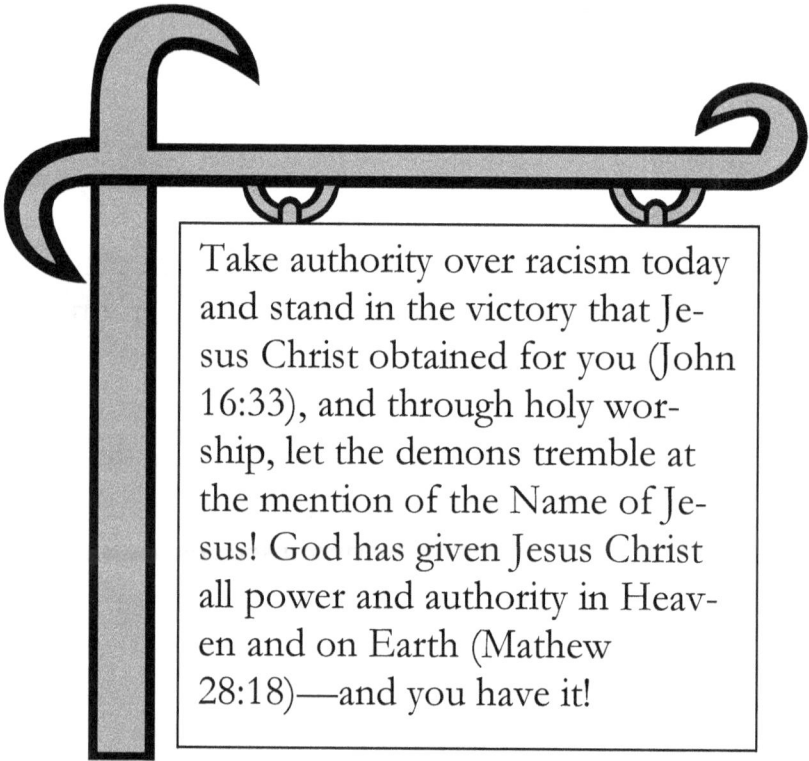

Take authority over racism today and stand in the victory that Jesus Christ obtained for you (John 16:33), and through holy worship, let the demons tremble at the mention of the Name of Jesus! God has given Jesus Christ all power and authority in Heaven and on Earth (Mathew 28:18)—and you have it!

63

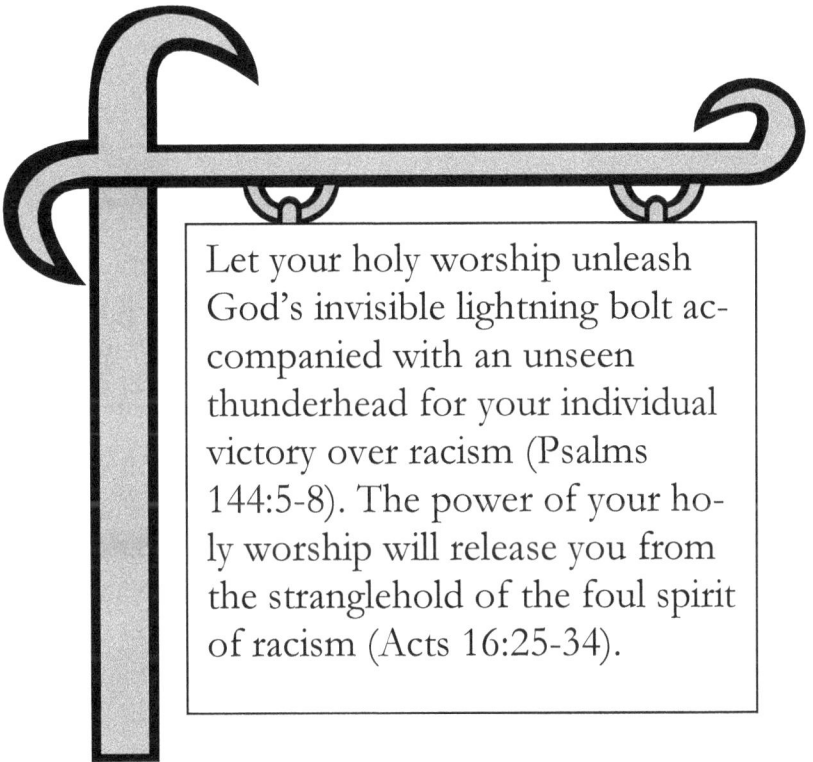

Let your holy worship unleash God's invisible lightning bolt accompanied with an unseen thunderhead for your individual victory over racism (Psalms 144:5-8). The power of your holy worship will release you from the stranglehold of the foul spirit of racism (Acts 16:25-34).

64

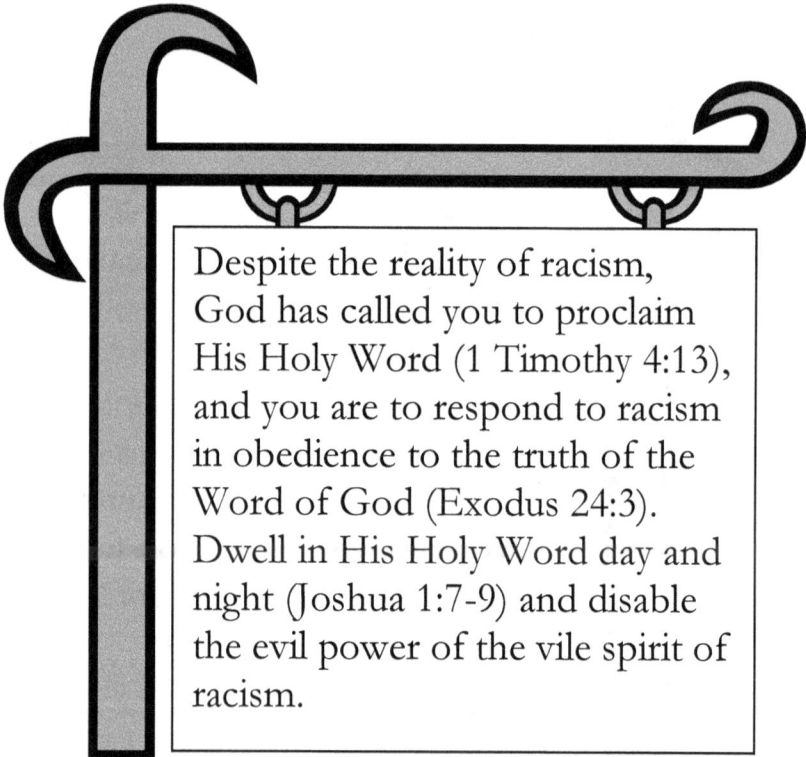

Despite the reality of racism, God has called you to proclaim His Holy Word (1 Timothy 4:13), and you are to respond to racism in obedience to the truth of the Word of God (Exodus 24:3). Dwell in His Holy Word day and night (Joshua 1:7-9) and disable the evil power of the vile spirit of racism.

65

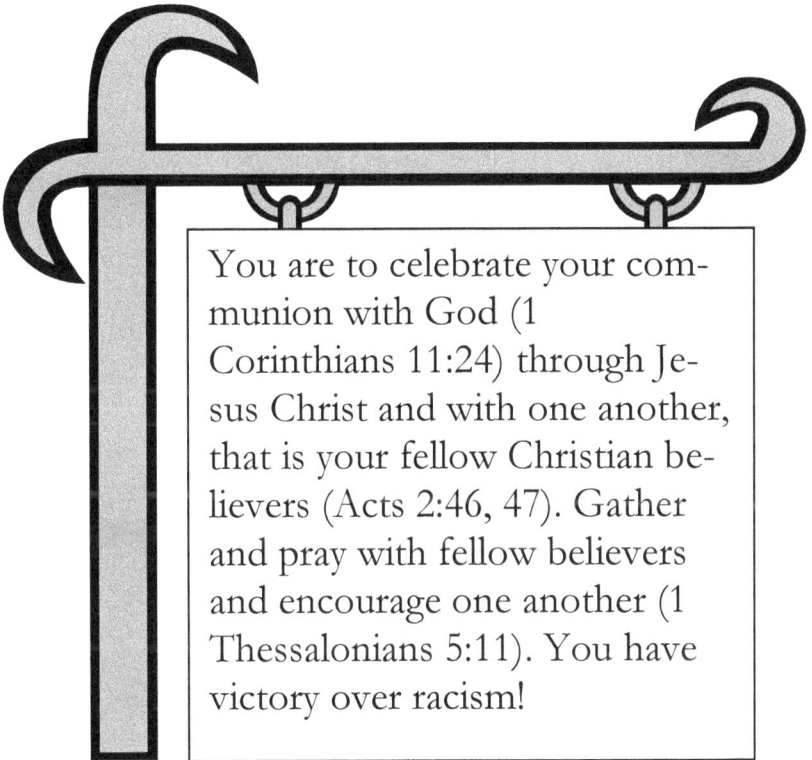

You are to celebrate your communion with God (1 Corinthians 11:24) through Jesus Christ and with one another, that is your fellow Christian believers (Acts 2:46, 47). Gather and pray with fellow believers and encourage one another (1 Thessalonians 5:11). You have victory over racism!

66

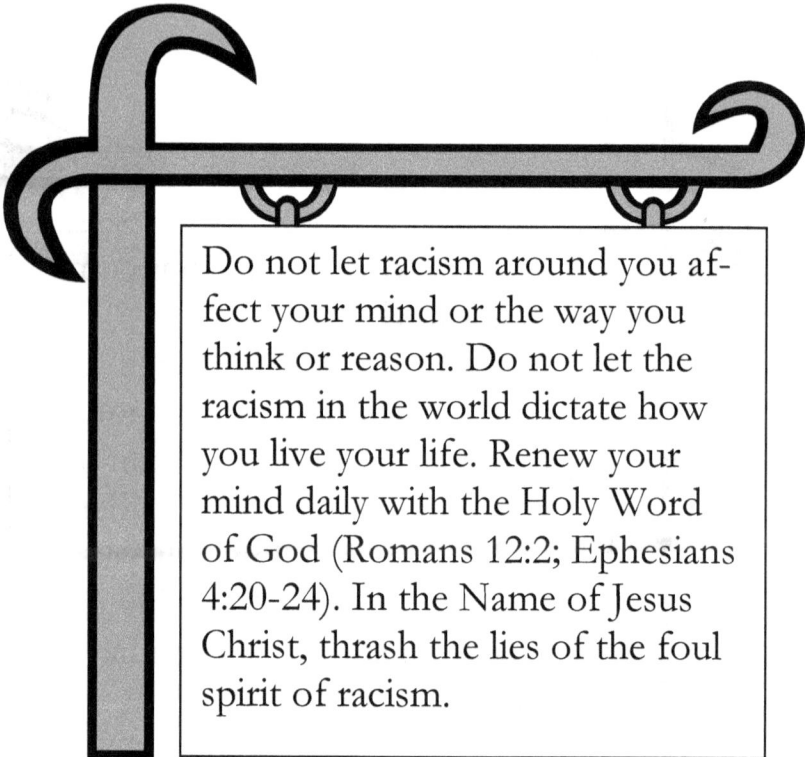

Do not let racism around you affect your mind or the way you think or reason. Do not let the racism in the world dictate how you live your life. Renew your mind daily with the Holy Word of God (Romans 12:2; Ephesians 4:20-24). In the Name of Jesus Christ, thrash the lies of the foul spirit of racism.

67

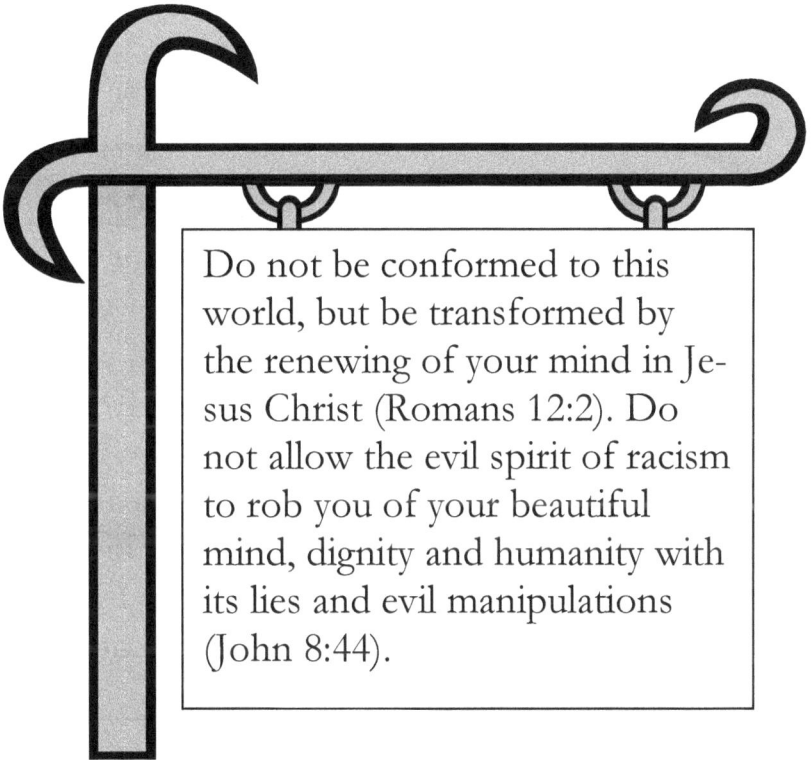

Do not be conformed to this world, but be transformed by the renewing of your mind in Jesus Christ (Romans 12:2). Do not allow the evil spirit of racism to rob you of your beautiful mind, dignity and humanity with its lies and evil manipulations (John 8:44).

68

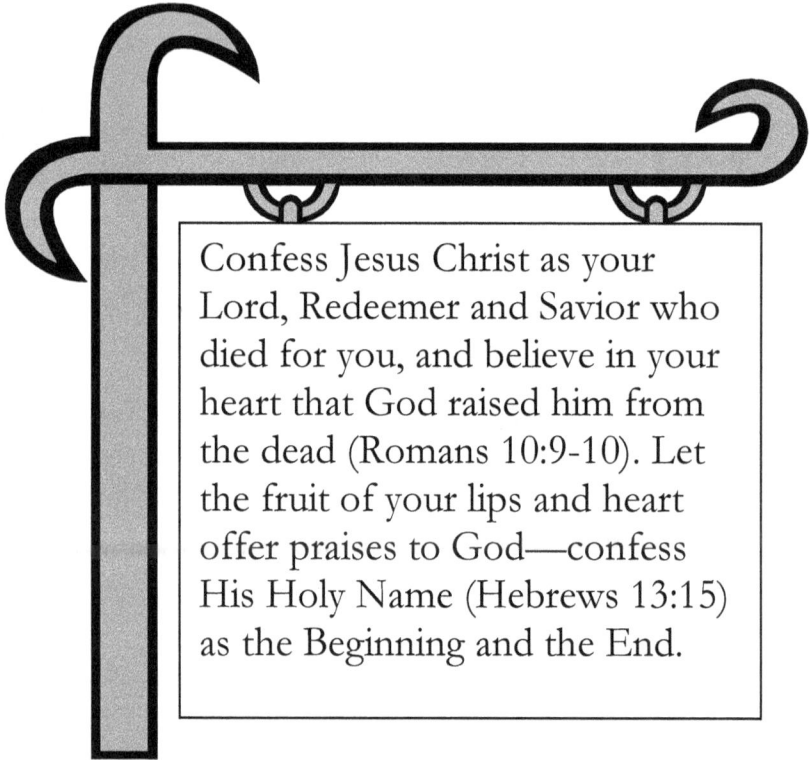

Confess Jesus Christ as your Lord, Redeemer and Savior who died for you, and believe in your heart that God raised him from the dead (Romans 10:9-10). Let the fruit of your lips and heart offer praises to God—confess His Holy Name (Hebrews 13:15) as the Beginning and the End.

69

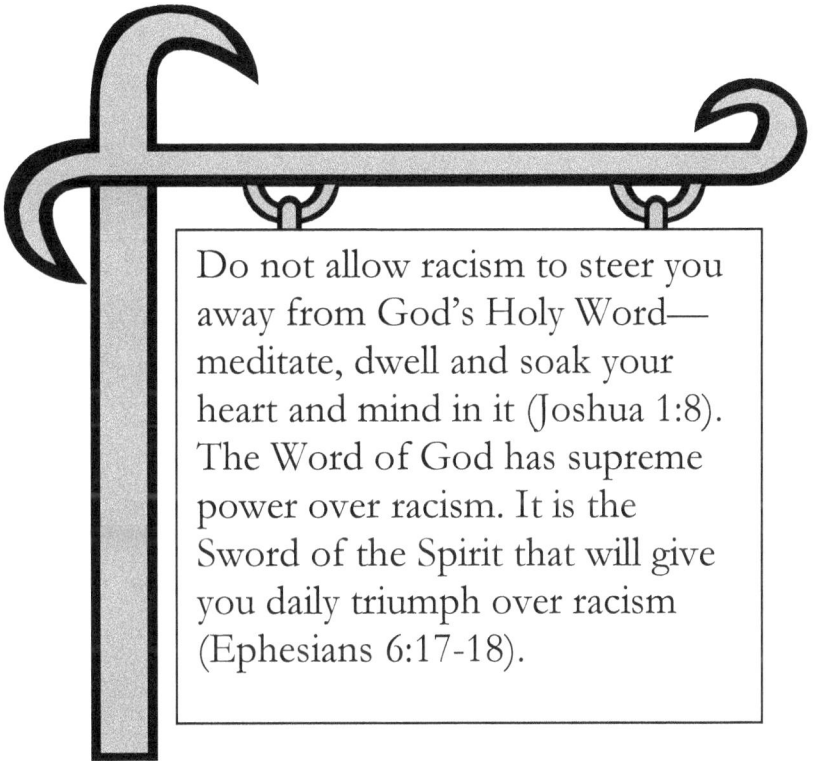

Do not allow racism to steer you away from God's Holy Word— meditate, dwell and soak your heart and mind in it (Joshua 1:8). The Word of God has supreme power over racism. It is the Sword of the Spirit that will give you daily triumph over racism (Ephesians 6:17-18).

70

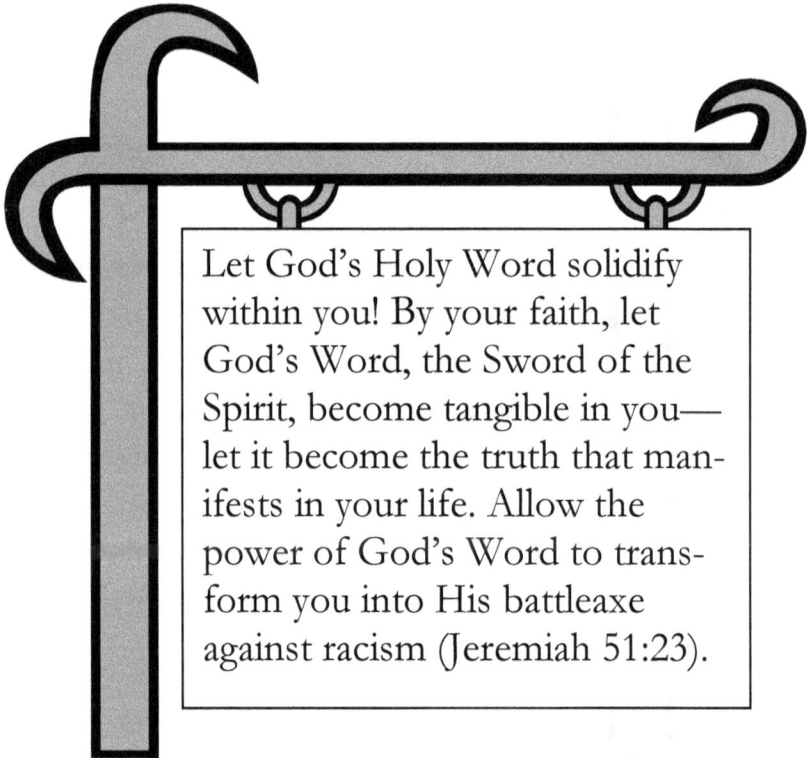

Let God's Holy Word solidify within you! By your faith, let God's Word, the Sword of the Spirit, become tangible in you— let it become the truth that manifests in your life. Allow the power of God's Word to transform you into His battleaxe against racism (Jeremiah 51:23).

71

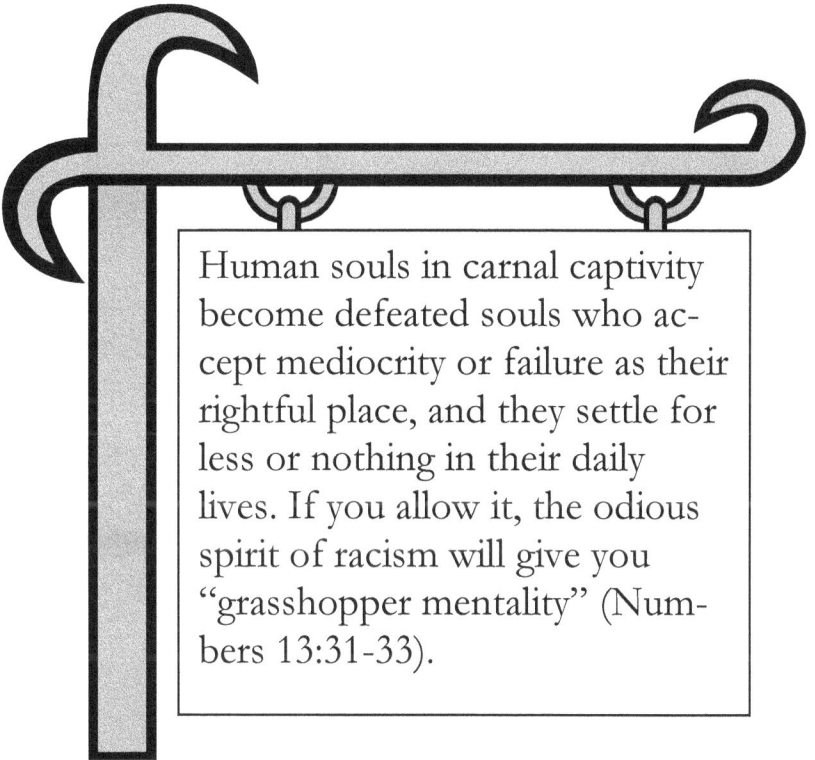

Human souls in carnal captivity become defeated souls who accept mediocrity or failure as their rightful place, and they settle for less or nothing in their daily lives. If you allow it, the odious spirit of racism will give you "grasshopper mentality" (Numbers 13:31-33).

72

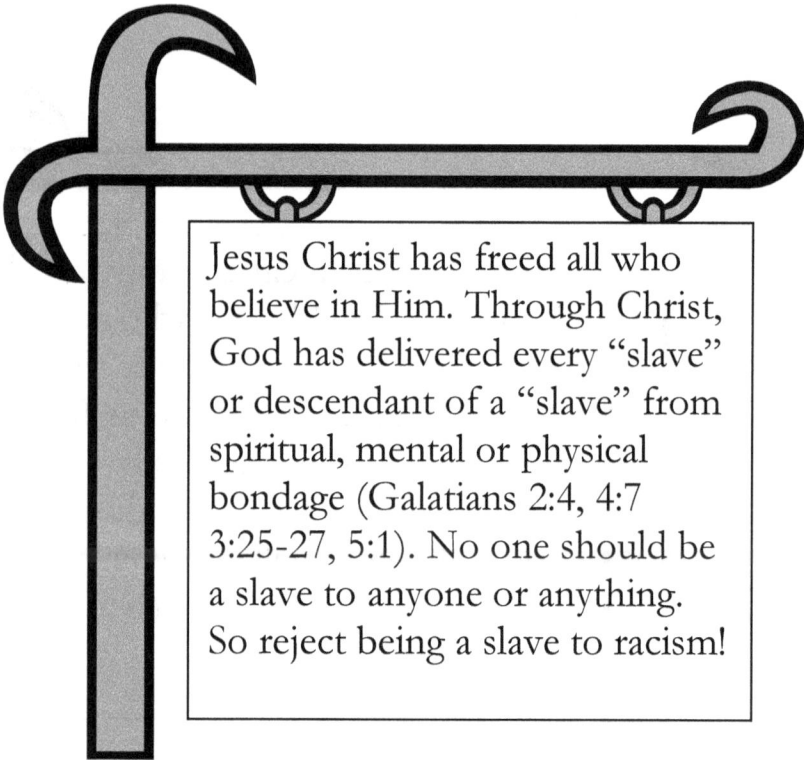

Jesus Christ has freed all who believe in Him. Through Christ, God has delivered every "slave" or descendant of a "slave" from spiritual, mental or physical bondage (Galatians 2:4, 4:7 3:25-27, 5:1). No one should be a slave to anyone or anything. So reject being a slave to racism!

73

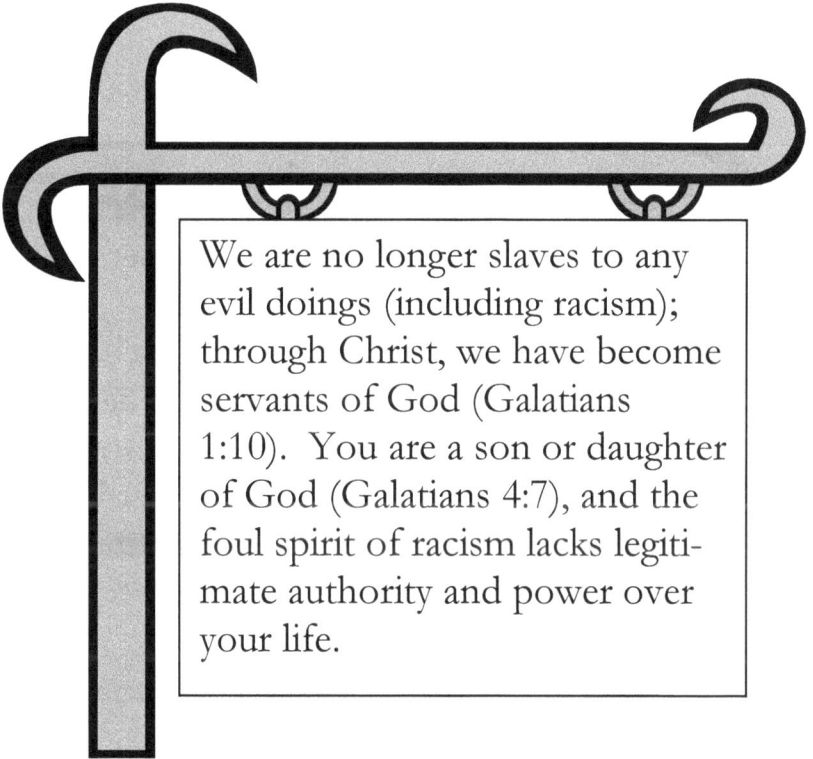

We are no longer slaves to any evil doings (including racism); through Christ, we have become servants of God (Galatians 1:10). You are a son or daughter of God (Galatians 4:7), and the foul spirit of racism lacks legitimate authority and power over your life.

74

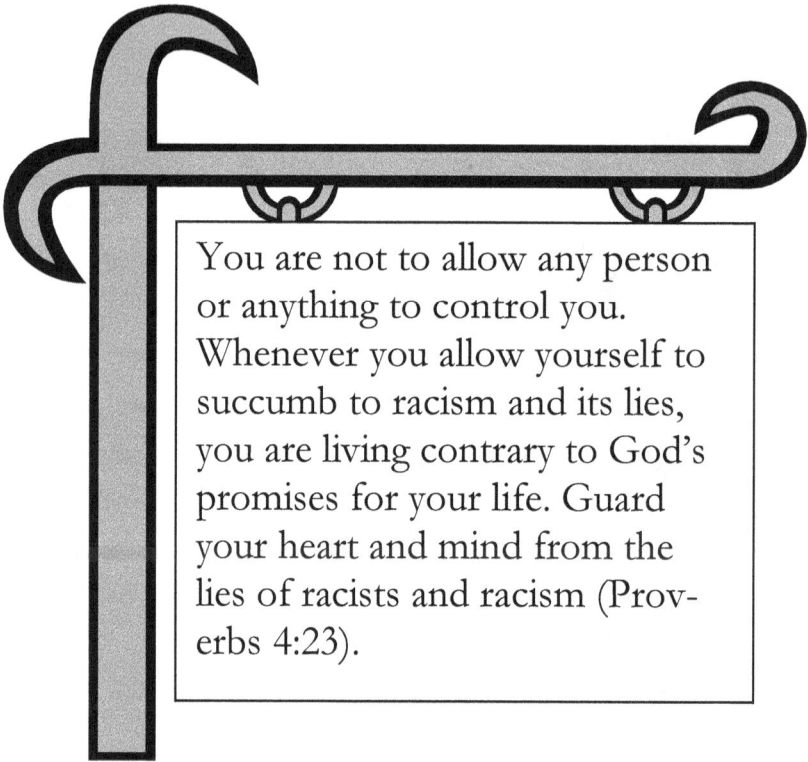

You are not to allow any person or anything to control you. Whenever you allow yourself to succumb to racism and its lies, you are living contrary to God's promises for your life. Guard your heart and mind from the lies of racists and racism (Proverbs 4:23).

75

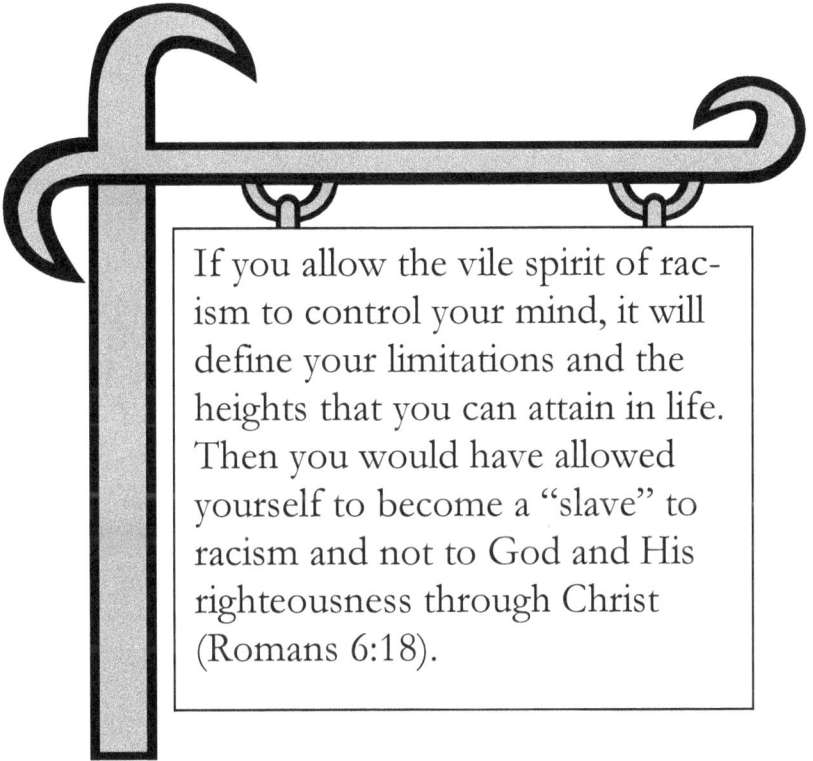

If you allow the vile spirit of racism to control your mind, it will define your limitations and the heights that you can attain in life. Then you would have allowed yourself to become a "slave" to racism and not to God and His righteousness through Christ (Romans 6:18).

76

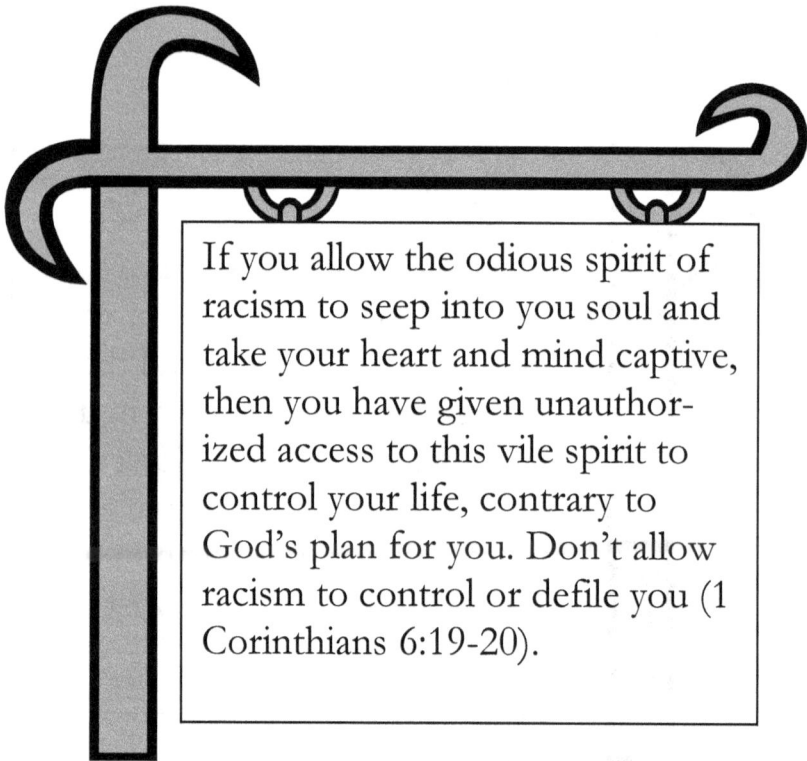

If you allow the odious spirit of racism to seep into you soul and take your heart and mind captive, then you have given unauthor- ized access to this vile spirit to control your life, contrary to God's plan for you. Don't allow racism to control or defile you (1 Corinthians 6:19-20).

77

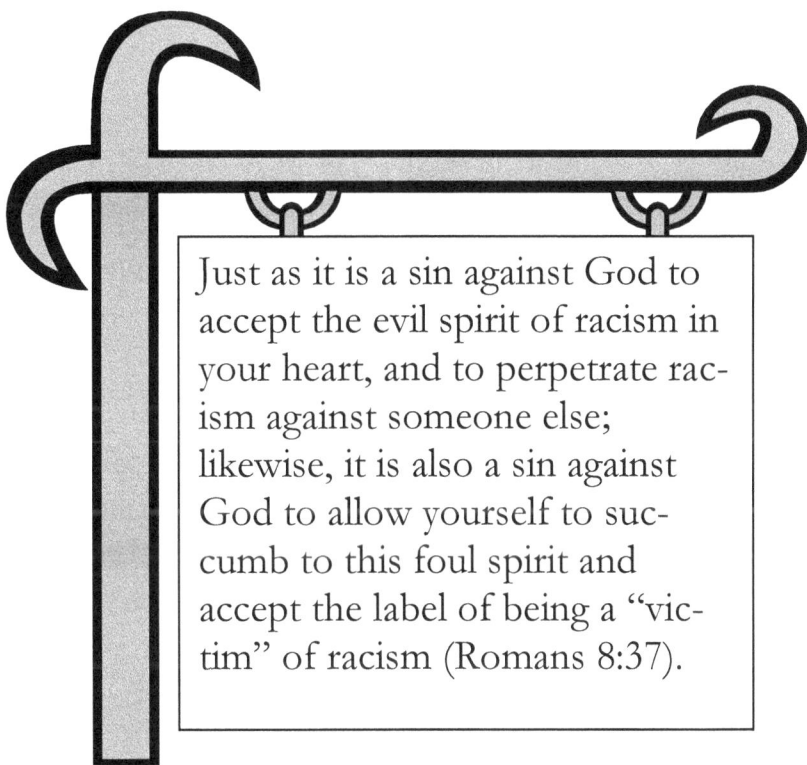

Just as it is a sin against God to accept the evil spirit of racism in your heart, and to perpetrate racism against someone else; likewise, it is also a sin against God to allow yourself to succumb to this foul spirit and accept the label of being a "victim" of racism (Romans 8:37).

78

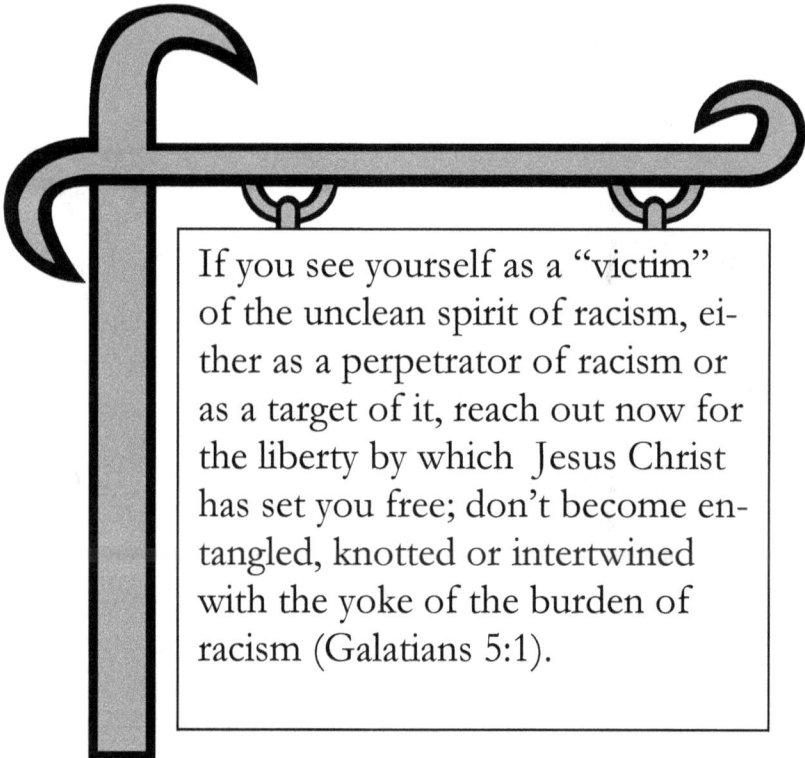

If you see yourself as a "victim" of the unclean spirit of racism, either as a perpetrator of racism or as a target of it, reach out now for the liberty by which Jesus Christ has set you free; don't become entangled, knotted or intertwined with the yoke of the burden of racism (Galatians 5:1).

79

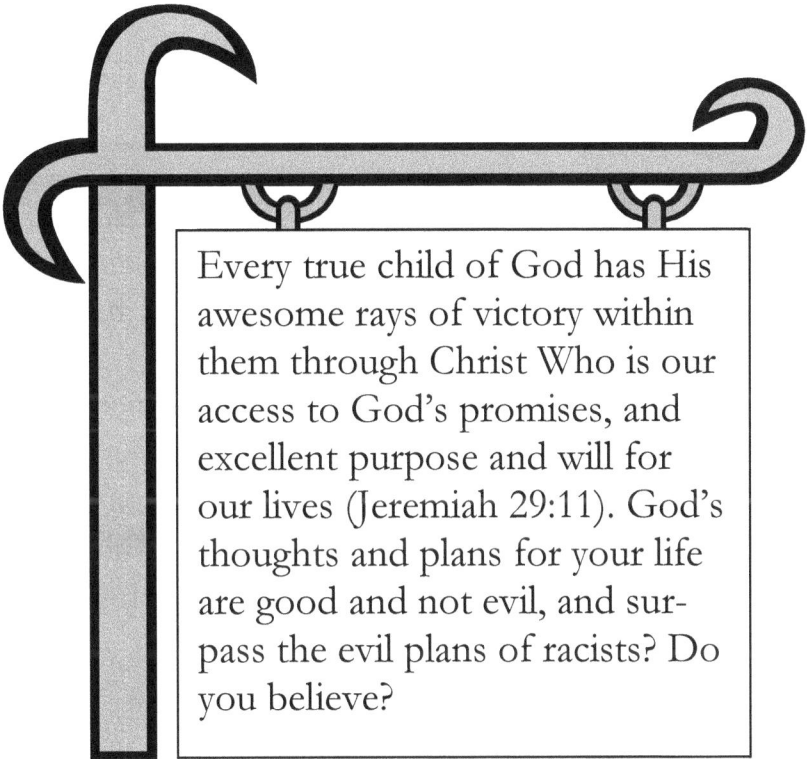

Every true child of God has His awesome rays of victory within them through Christ Who is our access to God's promises, and excellent purpose and will for our lives (Jeremiah 29:11). God's thoughts and plans for your life are good and not evil, and surpass the evil plans of racists? Do you believe?

80

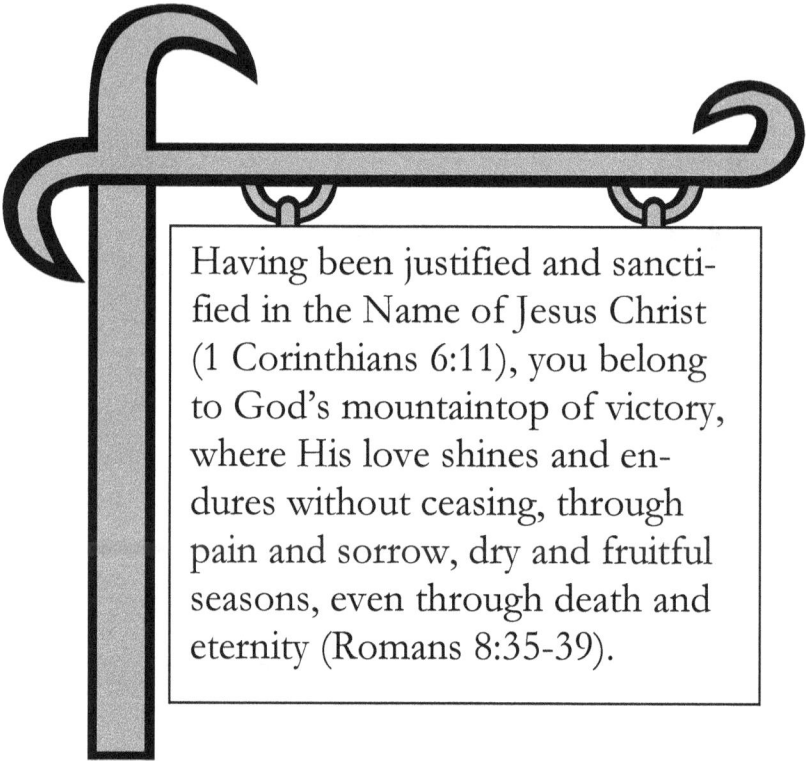

Having been justified and sanctified in the Name of Jesus Christ (1 Corinthians 6:11), you belong to God's mountaintop of victory, where His love shines and endures without ceasing, through pain and sorrow, dry and fruitful seasons, even through death and eternity (Romans 8:35-39).

81

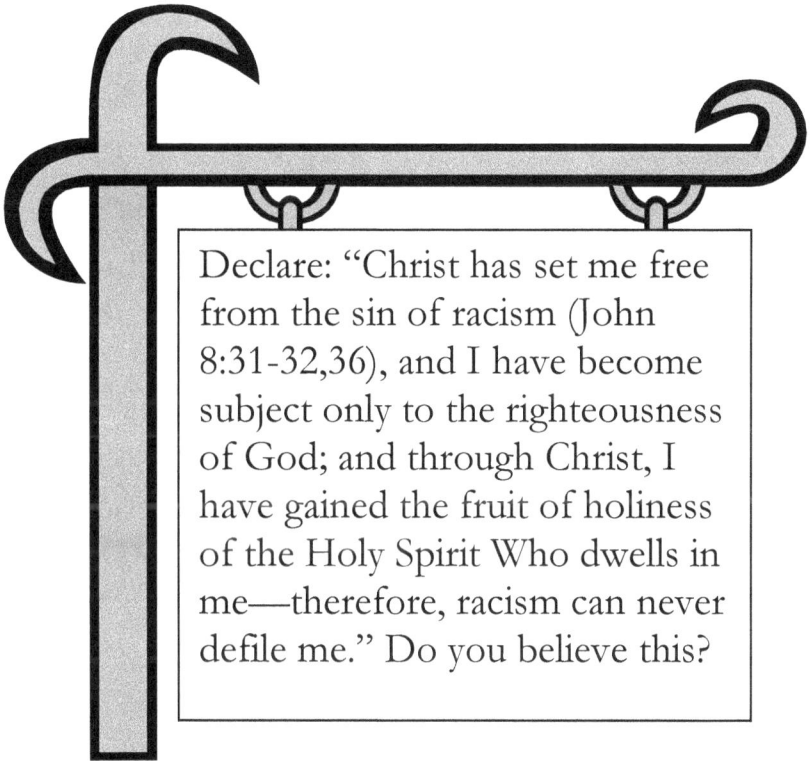

Declare: "Christ has set me free from the sin of racism (John 8:31-32,36), and I have become subject only to the righteousness of God; and through Christ, I have gained the fruit of holiness of the Holy Spirit Who dwells in me—therefore, racism can never defile me." Do you believe this?

82

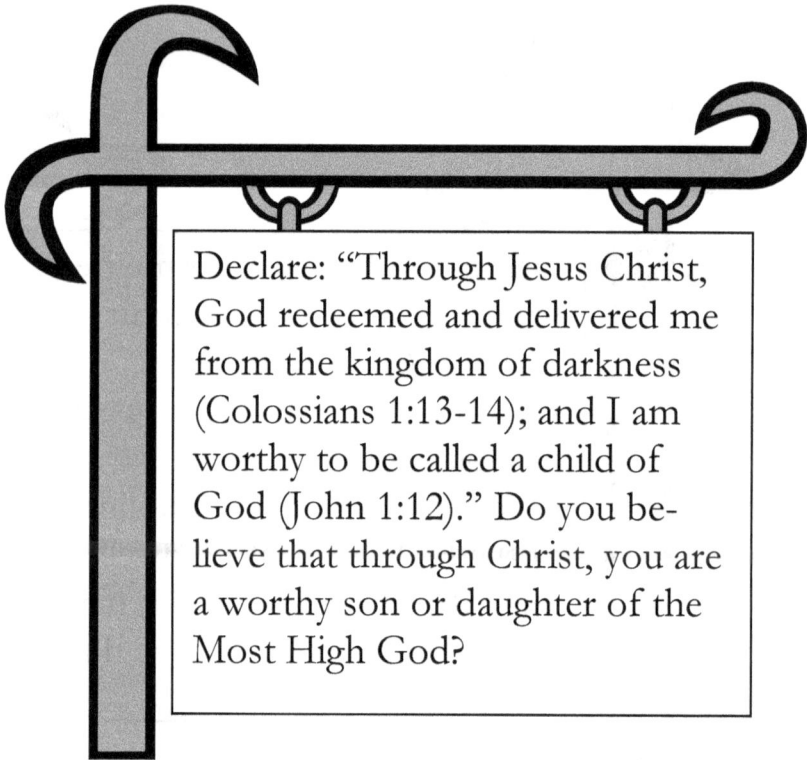

Declare: "Through Jesus Christ, God redeemed and delivered me from the kingdom of darkness (Colossians 1:13-14); and I am worthy to be called a child of God (John 1:12)." Do you believe that through Christ, you are a worthy son or daughter of the Most High God?

83

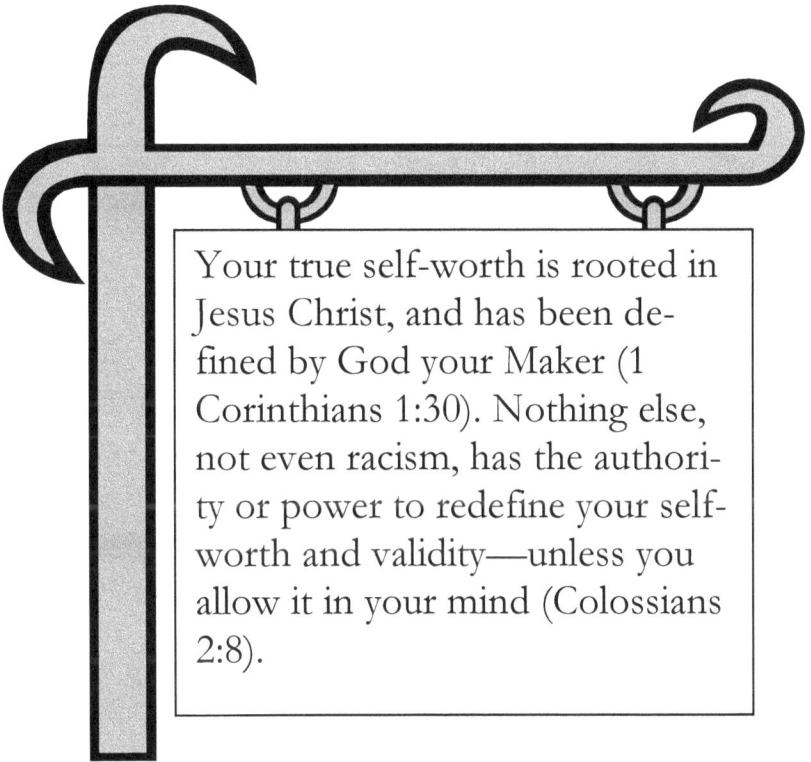

Your true self-worth is rooted in Jesus Christ, and has been defined by God your Maker (1 Corinthians 1:30). Nothing else, not even racism, has the authority or power to redefine your self-worth and validity—unless you allow it in your mind (Colossians 2:8).

84

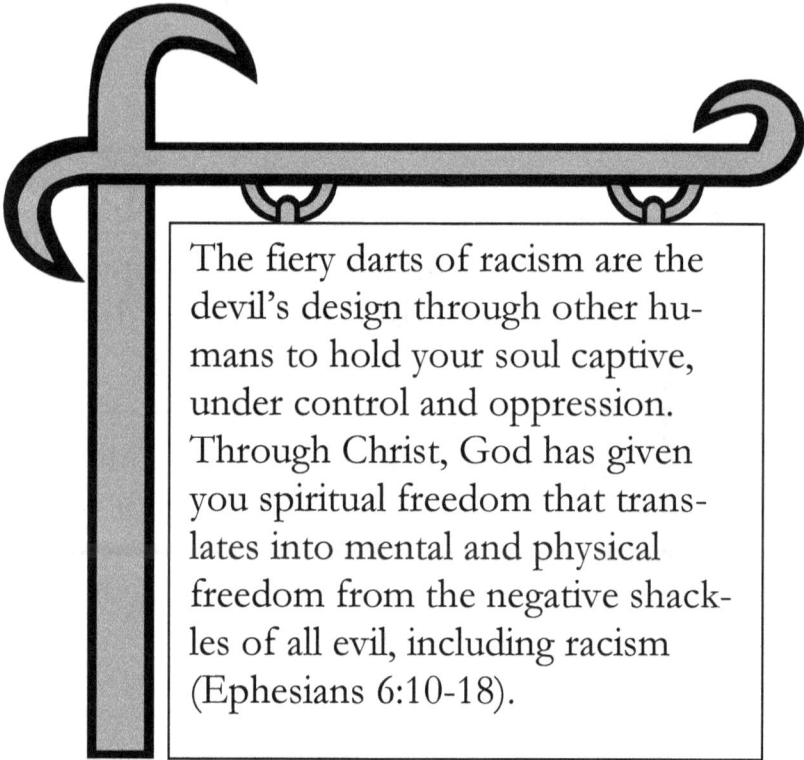

The fiery darts of racism are the devil's design through other humans to hold your soul captive, under control and oppression. Through Christ, God has given you spiritual freedom that translates into mental and physical freedom from the negative shackles of all evil, including racism (Ephesians 6:10-18).

85

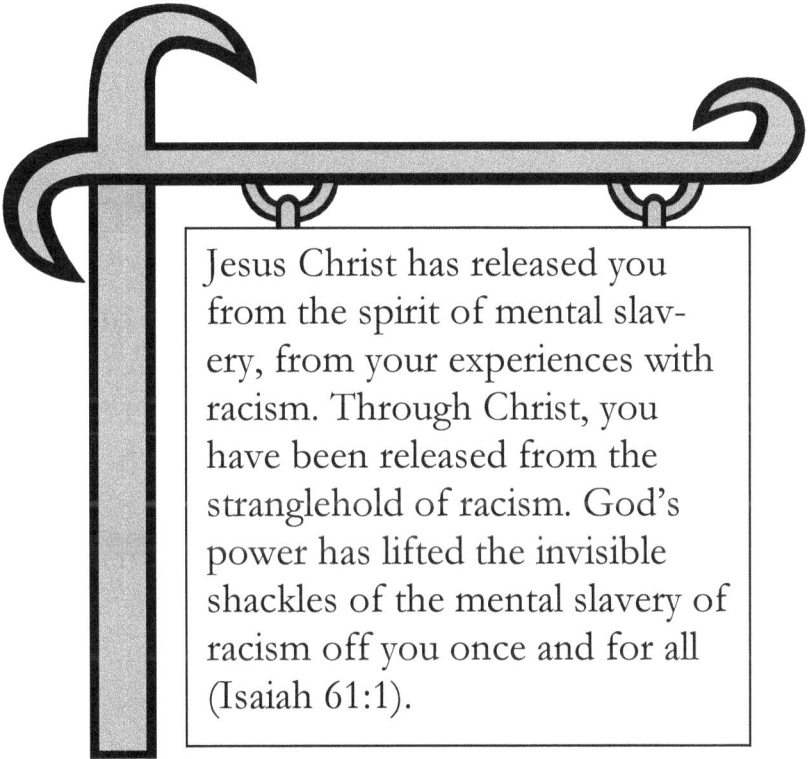

Jesus Christ has released you from the spirit of mental slavery, from your experiences with racism. Through Christ, you have been released from the stranglehold of racism. God's power has lifted the invisible shackles of the mental slavery of racism off you once and for all (Isaiah 61:1).

86

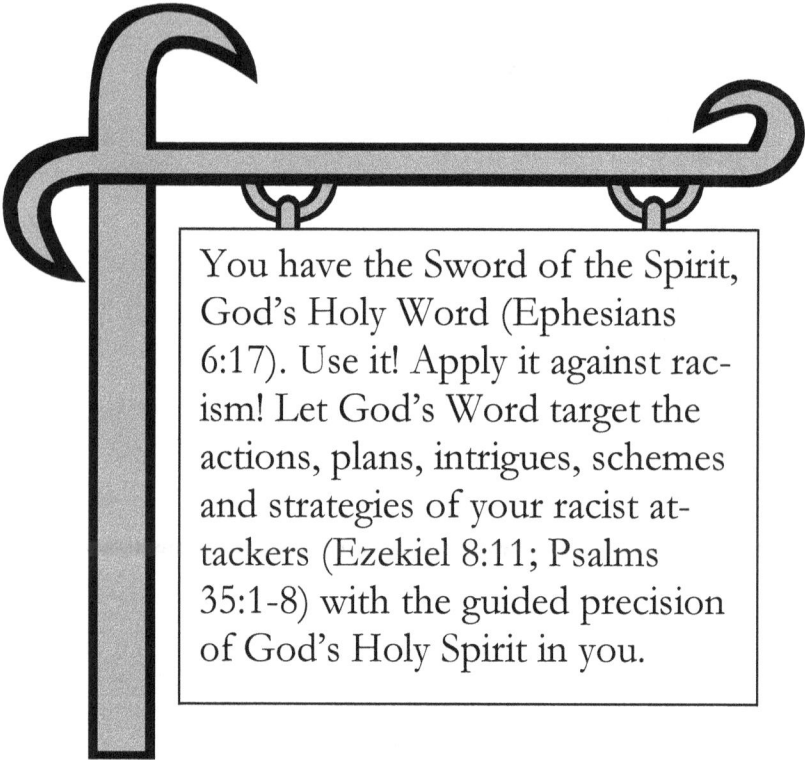

You have the Sword of the Spirit, God's Holy Word (Ephesians 6:17). Use it! Apply it against racism! Let God's Word target the actions, plans, intrigues, schemes and strategies of your racist attackers (Ezekiel 8:11; Psalms 35:1-8) with the guided precision of God's Holy Spirit in you.

87

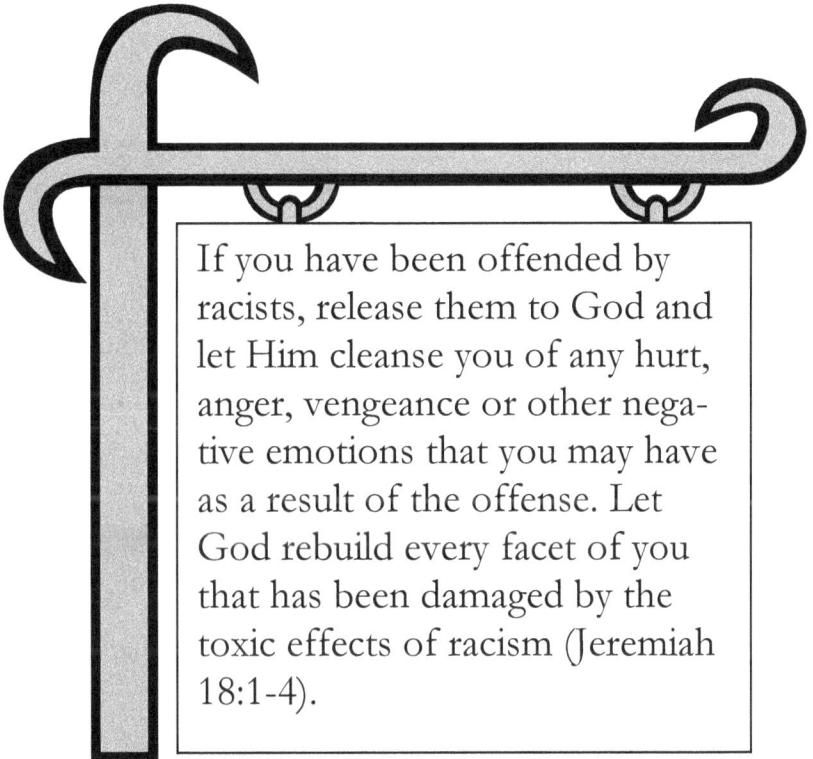

If you have been offended by racists, release them to God and let Him cleanse you of any hurt, anger, vengeance or other negative emotions that you may have as a result of the offense. Let God rebuild every facet of you that has been damaged by the toxic effects of racism (Jeremiah 18:1-4).

88

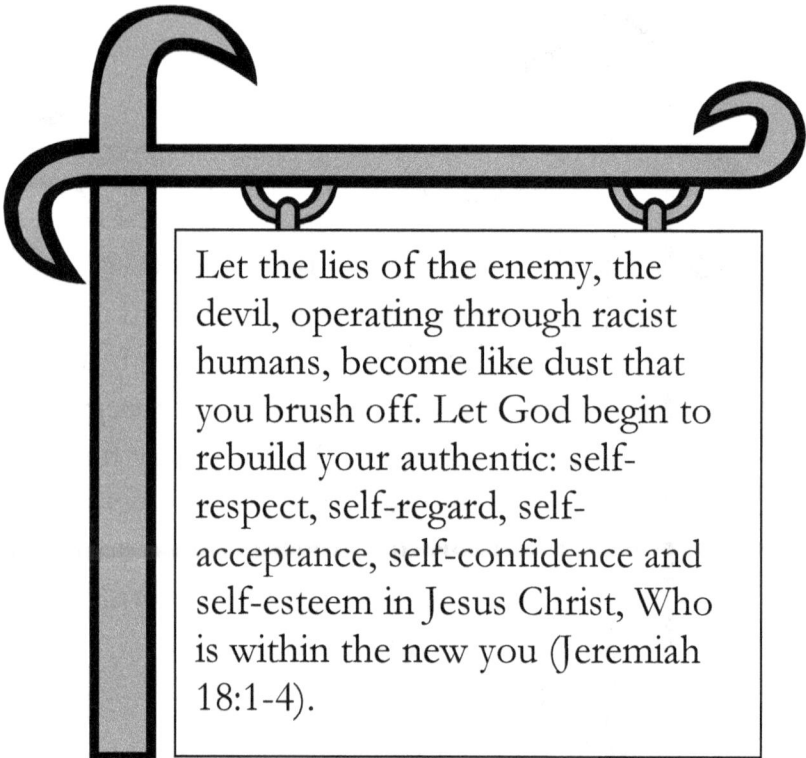

Let the lies of the enemy, the devil, operating through racist humans, become like dust that you brush off. Let God begin to rebuild your authentic: self-respect, self-regard, self-acceptance, self-confidence and self-esteem in Jesus Christ, Who is within the new you (Jeremiah 18:1-4).

89

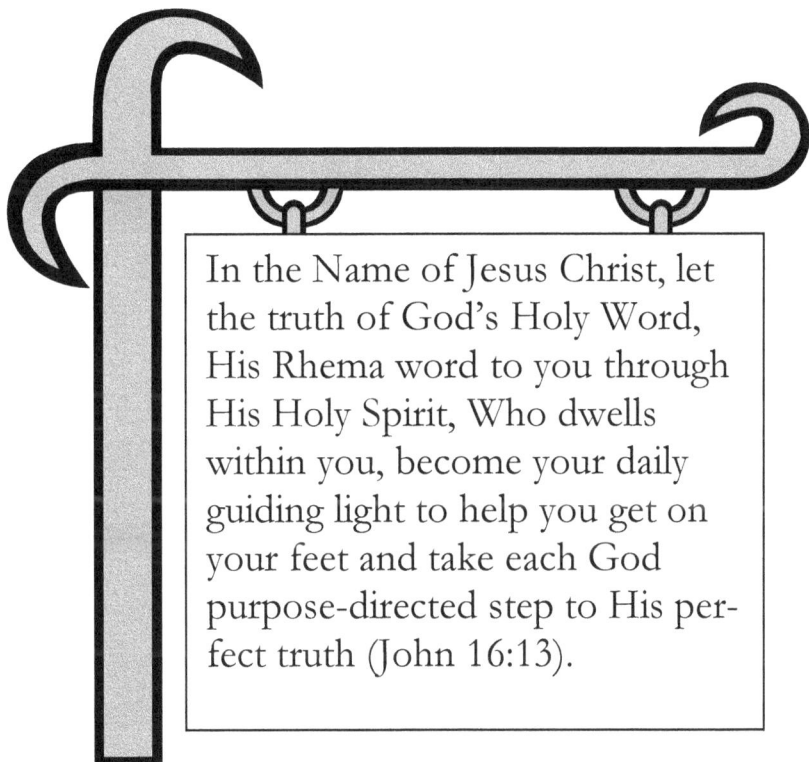

In the Name of Jesus Christ, let the truth of God's Holy Word, His Rhema word to you through His Holy Spirit, Who dwells within you, become your daily guiding light to help you get on your feet and take each God purpose-directed step to His perfect truth (John 16:13).

90

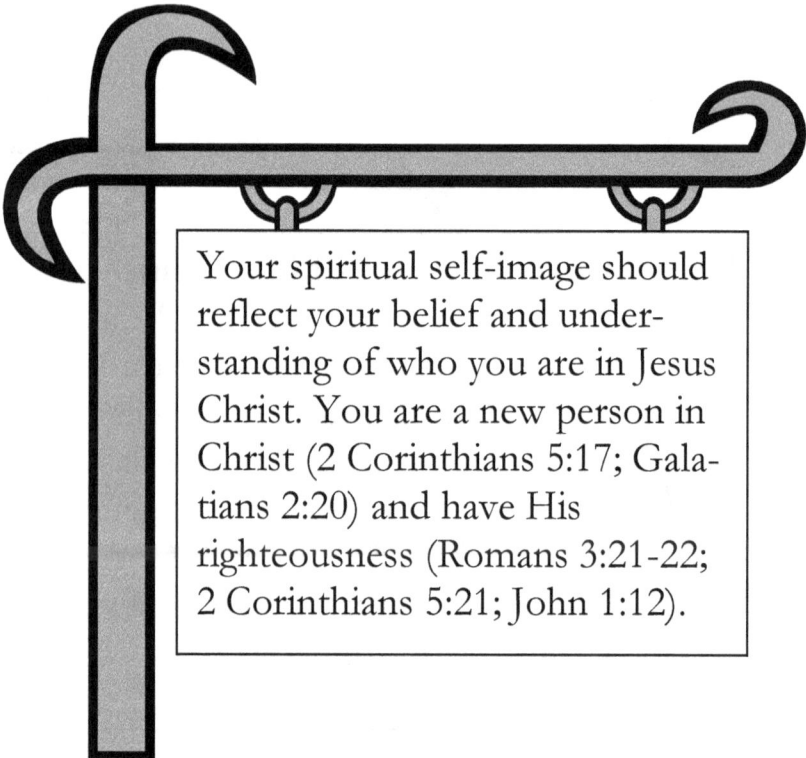

Your spiritual self-image should reflect your belief and understanding of who you are in Jesus Christ. You are a new person in Christ (2 Corinthians 5:17; Galatians 2:20) and have His righteousness (Romans 3:21-22; 2 Corinthians 5:21; John 1:12).

91

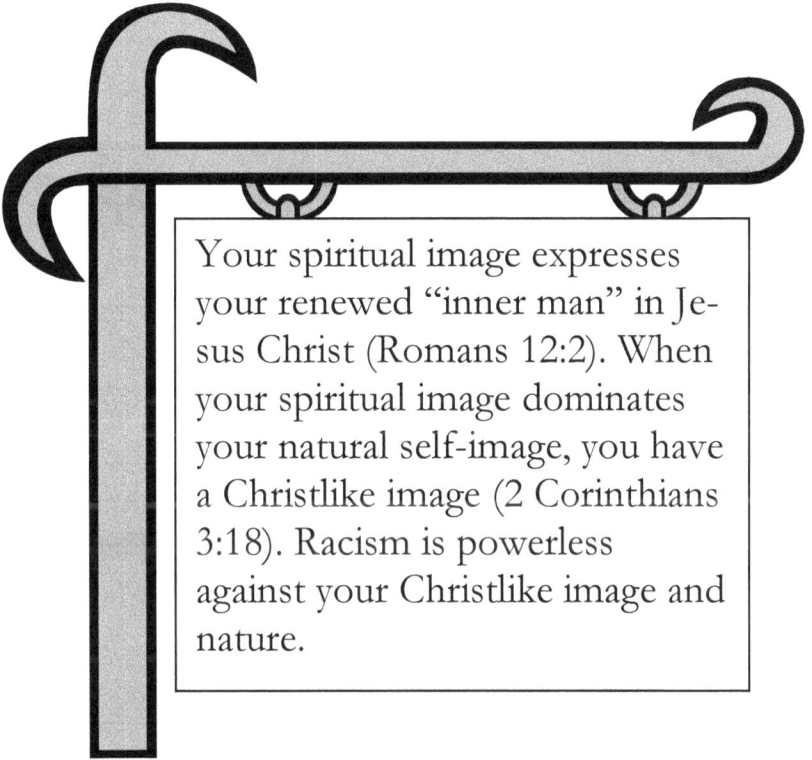

Your spiritual image expresses your renewed "inner man" in Jesus Christ (Romans 12:2). When your spiritual image dominates your natural self-image, you have a Christlike image (2 Corinthians 3:18). Racism is powerless against your Christlike image and nature.

92

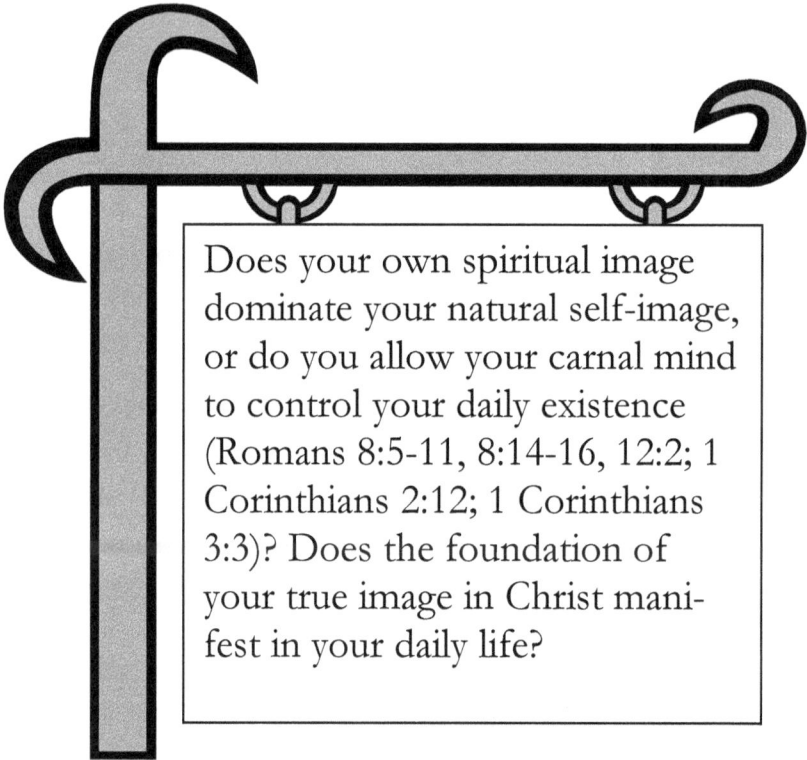

Does your own spiritual image dominate your natural self-image, or do you allow your carnal mind to control your daily existence (Romans 8:5-11, 8:14-16, 12:2; 1 Corinthians 2:12; 1 Corinthians 3:3)? Does the foundation of your true image in Christ manifest in your daily life?

93

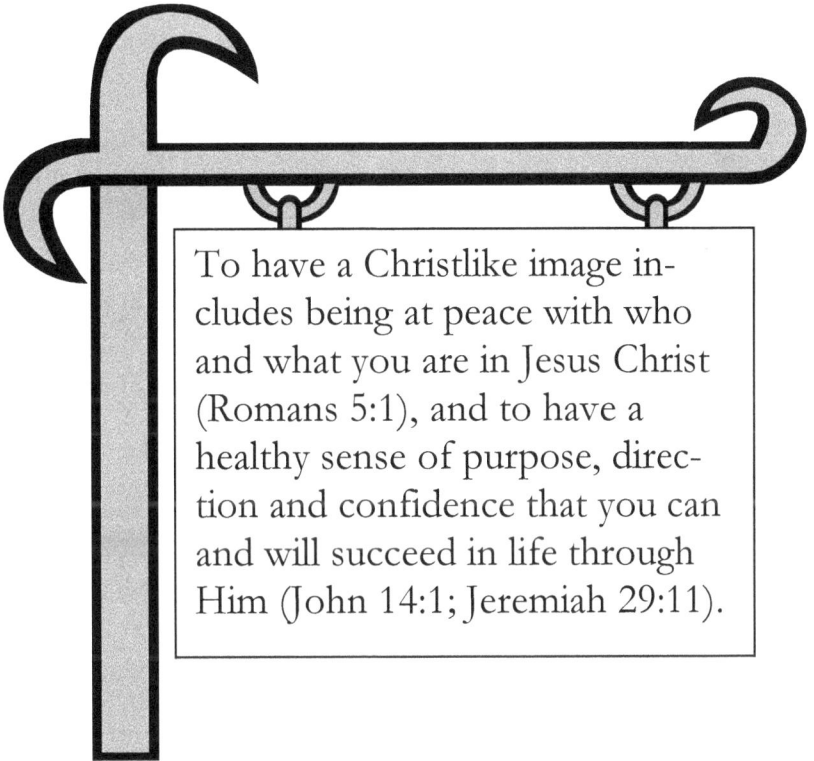

To have a Christlike image includes being at peace with who and what you are in Jesus Christ (Romans 5:1), and to have a healthy sense of purpose, direction and confidence that you can and will succeed in life through Him (John 14:1; Jeremiah 29:11).

94

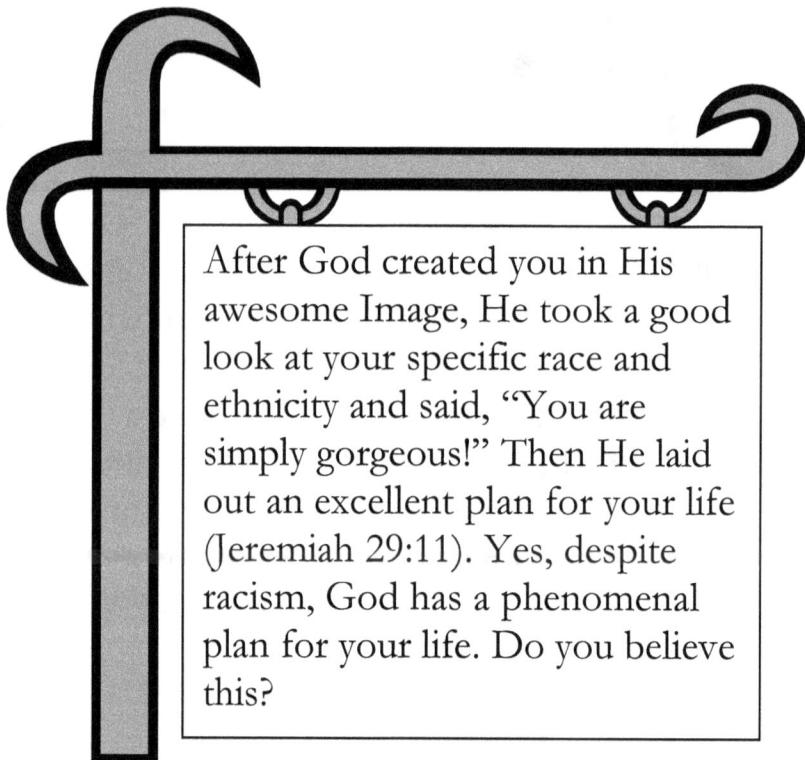

After God created you in His awesome Image, He took a good look at your specific race and ethnicity and said, "You are simply gorgeous!" Then He laid out an excellent plan for your life (Jeremiah 29:11). Yes, despite racism, God has a phenomenal plan for your life. Do you believe this?

95

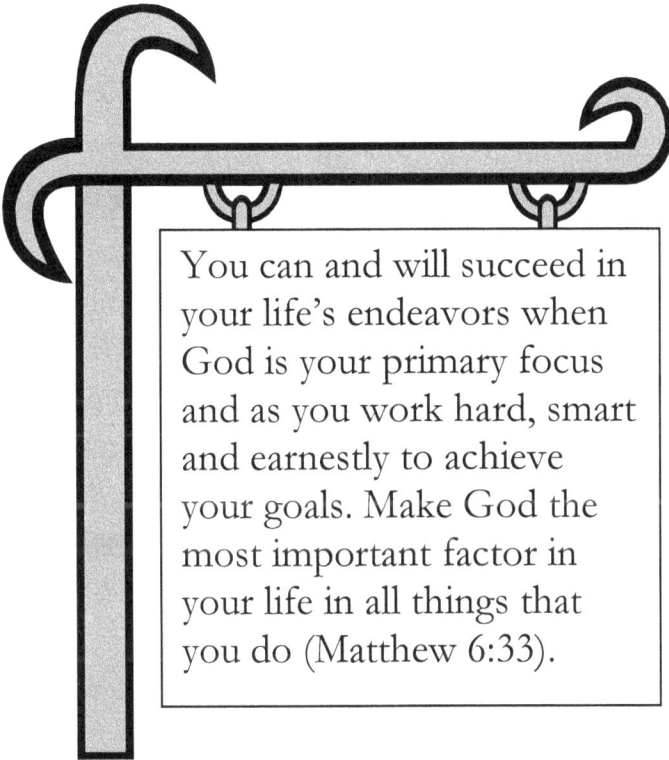

You can and will succeed in your life's endeavors when God is your primary focus and as you work hard, smart and earnestly to achieve your goals. Make God the most important factor in your life in all things that you do (Matthew 6:33).

96

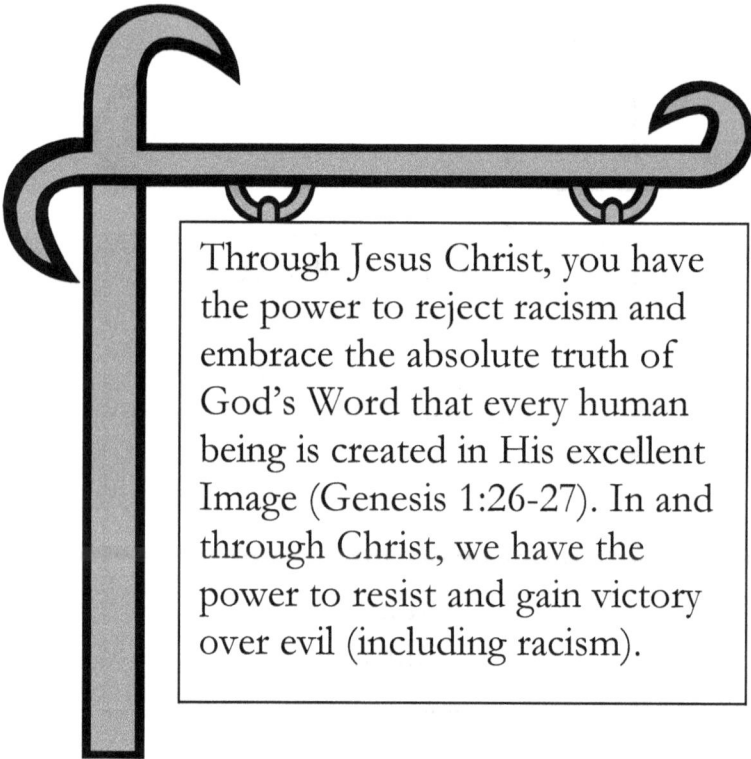

Through Jesus Christ, you have the power to reject racism and embrace the absolute truth of God's Word that every human being is created in His excellent Image (Genesis 1:26-27). In and through Christ, we have the power to resist and gain victory over evil (including racism).

97

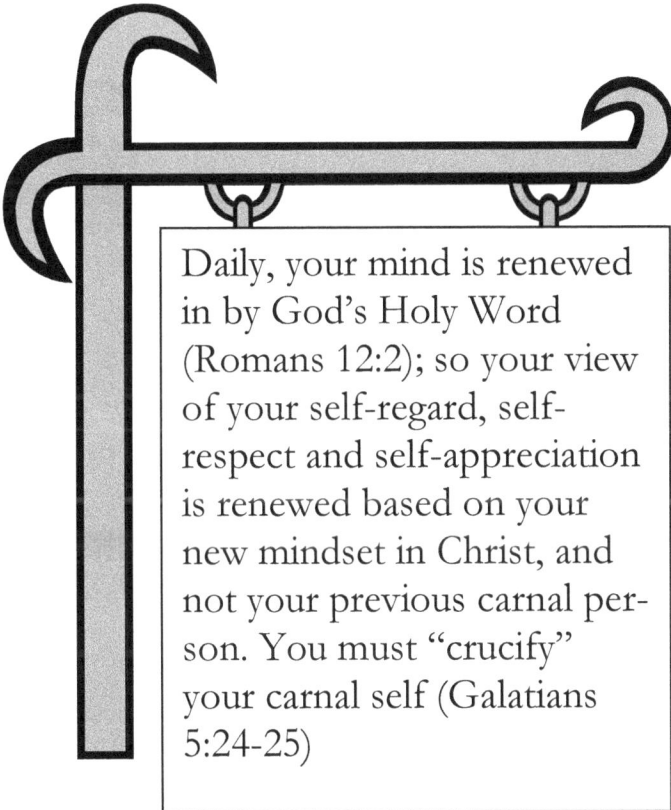

Daily, your mind is renewed in by God's Holy Word (Romans 12:2); so your view of your self-regard, self-respect and self-appreciation is renewed based on your new mindset in Christ, and not your previous carnal person. You must "crucify" your carnal self (Galatians 5:24-25)

98

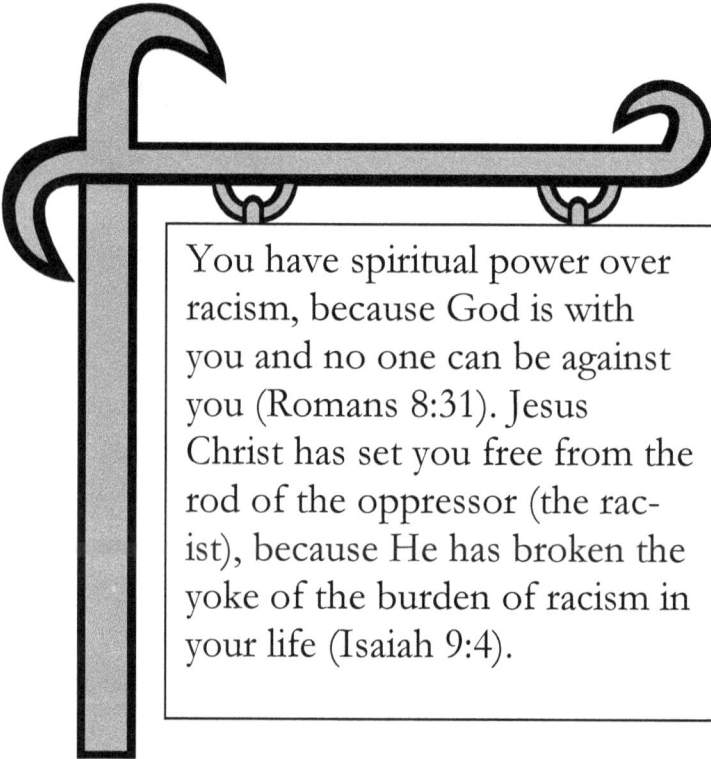

You have spiritual power over racism, because God is with you and no one can be against you (Romans 8:31). Jesus Christ has set you free from the rod of the oppressor (the racist), because He has broken the yoke of the burden of racism in your life (Isaiah 9:4).

99

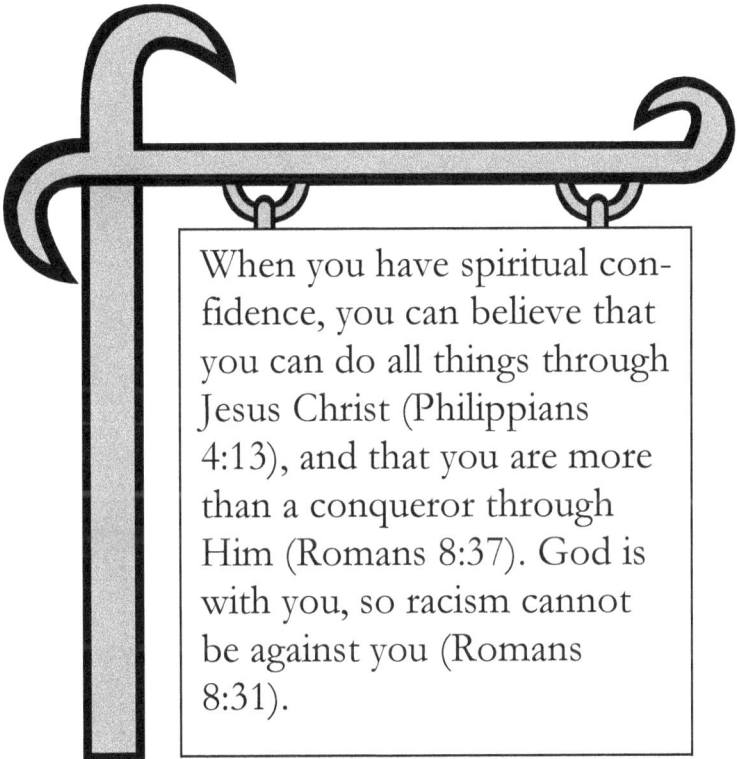

When you have spiritual confidence, you can believe that you can do all things through Jesus Christ (Philippians 4:13), and that you are more than a conqueror through Him (Romans 8:37). God is with you, so racism cannot be against you (Romans 8:31).

100

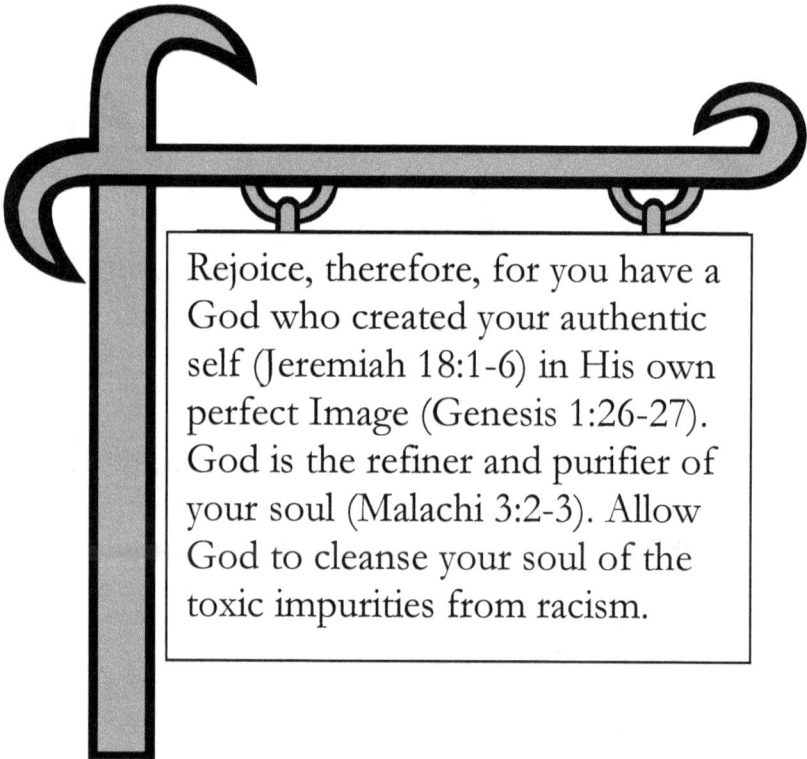

Rejoice, therefore, for you have a God who created your authentic self (Jeremiah 18:1-6) in His own perfect Image (Genesis 1:26-27). God is the refiner and purifier of your soul (Malachi 3:2-3). Allow God to cleanse your soul of the toxic impurities from racism.

101

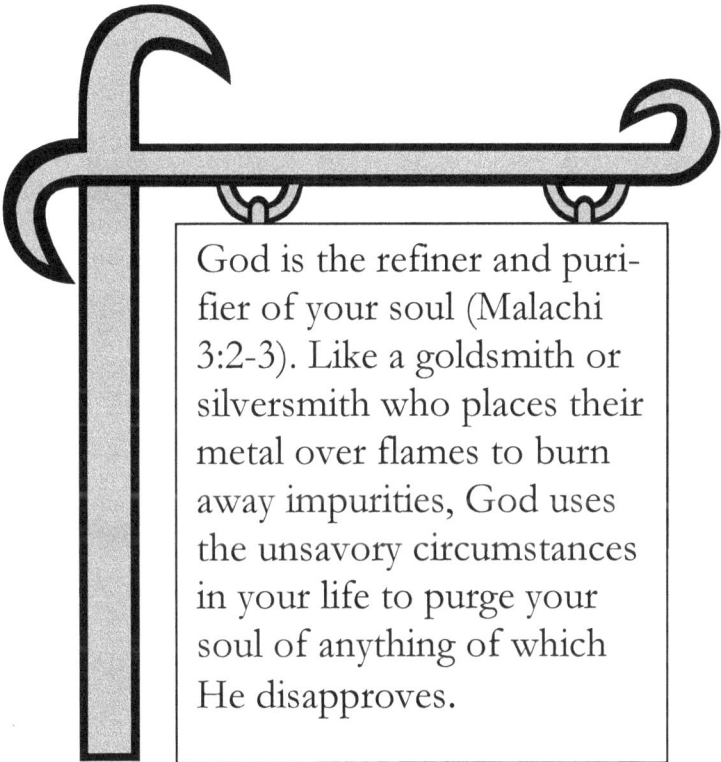

God is the refiner and purifier of your soul (Malachi 3:2-3). Like a goldsmith or silversmith who places their metal over flames to burn away impurities, God uses the unsavory circumstances in your life to purge your soul of anything of which He disapproves.

102

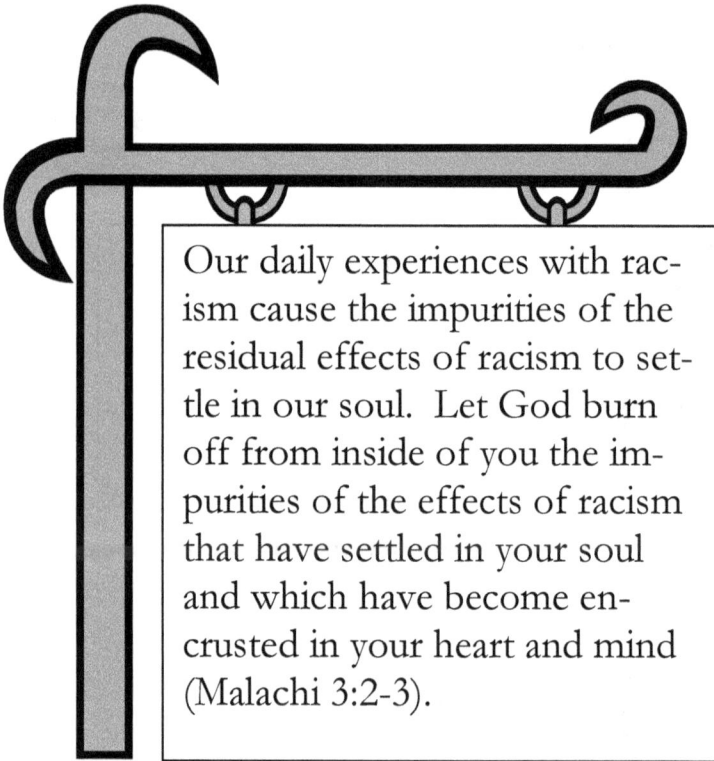

Our daily experiences with racism cause the impurities of the residual effects of racism to settle in our soul. Let God burn off from inside of you the impurities of the effects of racism that have settled in your soul and which have become encrusted in your heart and mind (Malachi 3:2-3).

103

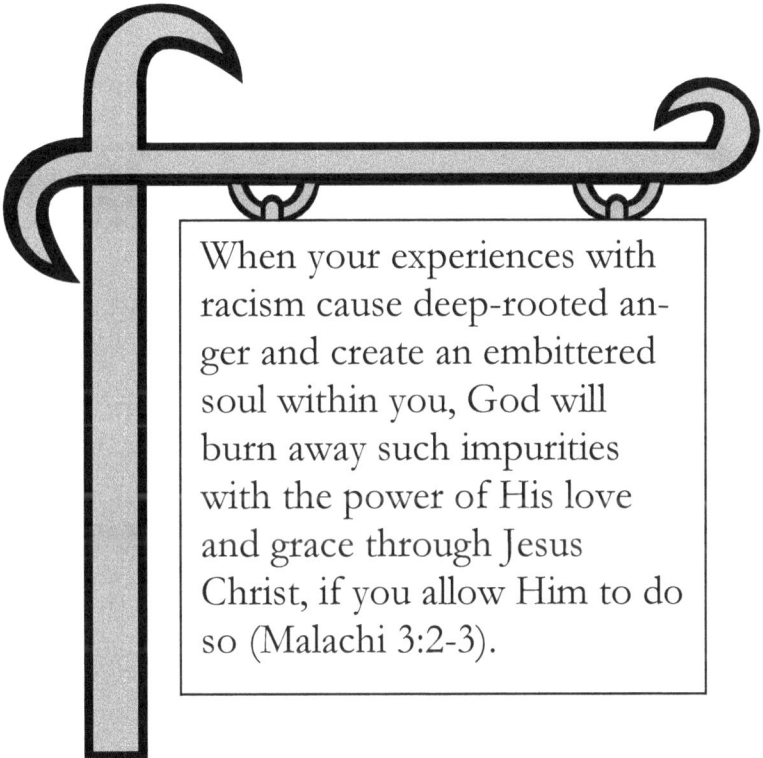

When your experiences with racism cause deep-rooted anger and create an embittered soul within you, God will burn away such impurities with the power of His love and grace through Jesus Christ, if you allow Him to do so (Malachi 3:2-3).

104

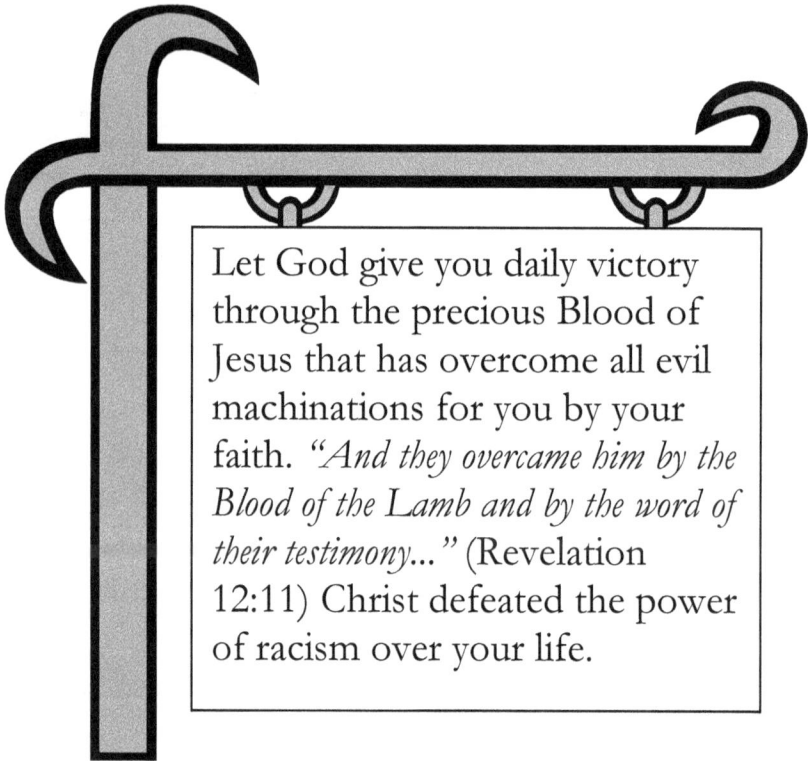

Let God give you daily victory through the precious Blood of Jesus that has overcome all evil machinations for you by your faith. *"And they overcame him by the Blood of the Lamb and by the word of their testimony..."* (Revelation 12:11) Christ defeated the power of racism over your life.

105

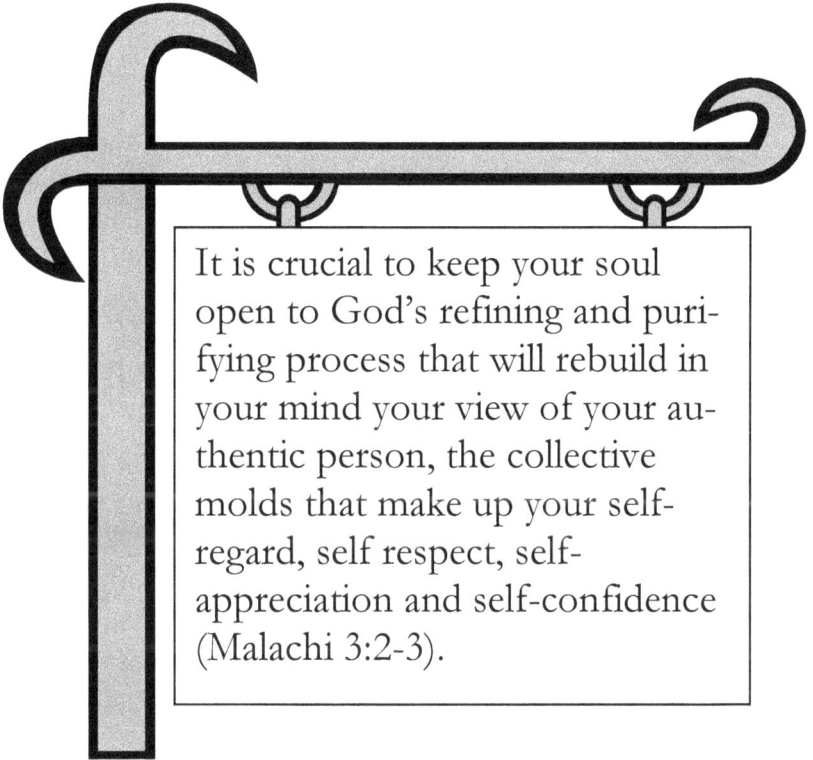

It is crucial to keep your soul open to God's refining and purifying process that will rebuild in your mind your view of your authentic person, the collective molds that make up your self-regard, self respect, self-appreciation and self-confidence (Malachi 3:2-3).

106

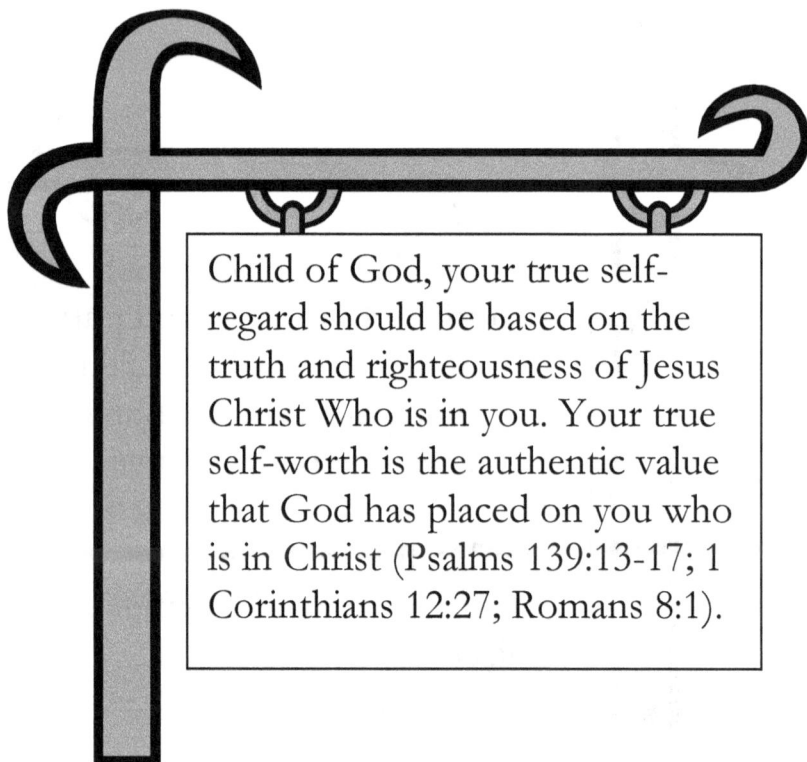

Child of God, your true self-regard should be based on the truth and righteousness of Jesus Christ Who is in you. Your true self-worth is the authentic value that God has placed on you who is in Christ (Psalms 139:13-17; 1 Corinthians 12:27; Romans 8:1).

107

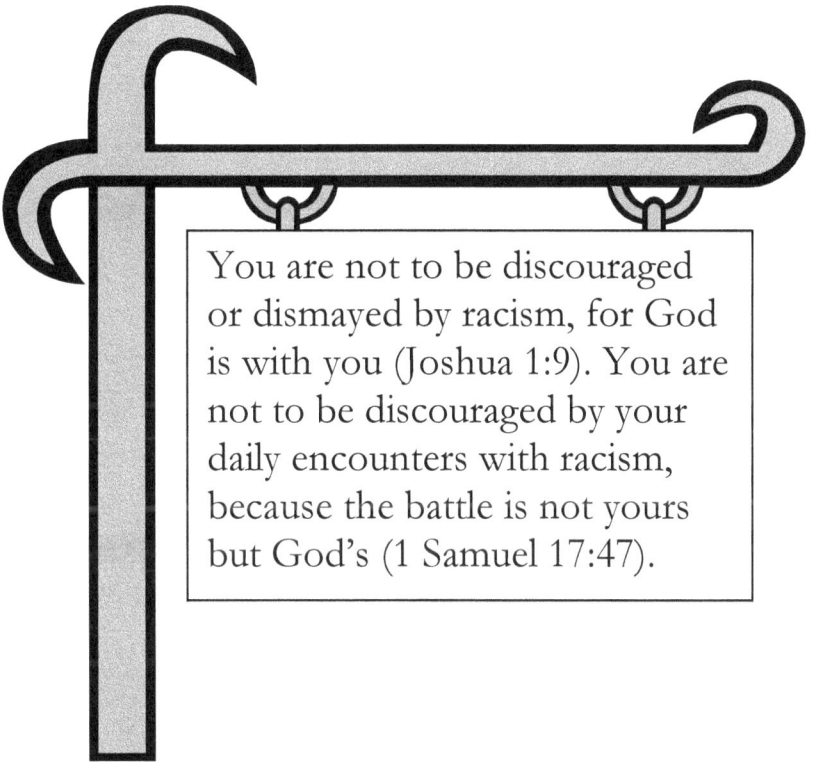

You are not to be discouraged or dismayed by racism, for God is with you (Joshua 1:9). You are not to be discouraged by your daily encounters with racism, because the battle is not yours but God's (1 Samuel 17:47).

108

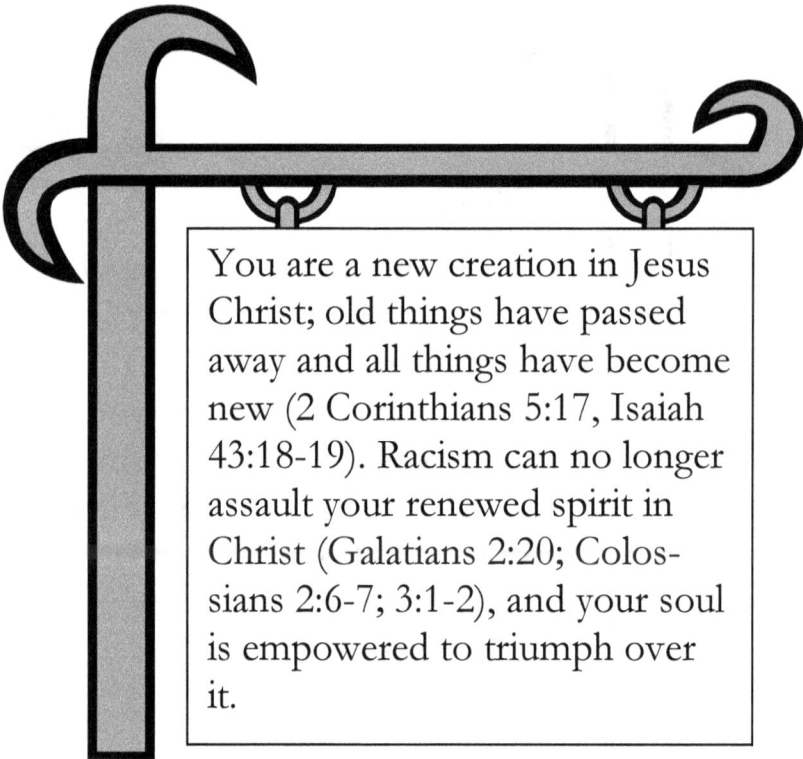

You are a new creation in Jesus Christ; old things have passed away and all things have become new (2 Corinthians 5:17, Isaiah 43:18-19). Racism can no longer assault your renewed spirit in Christ (Galatians 2:20; Colossians 2:6-7; 3:1-2), and your soul is empowered to triumph over it.

109

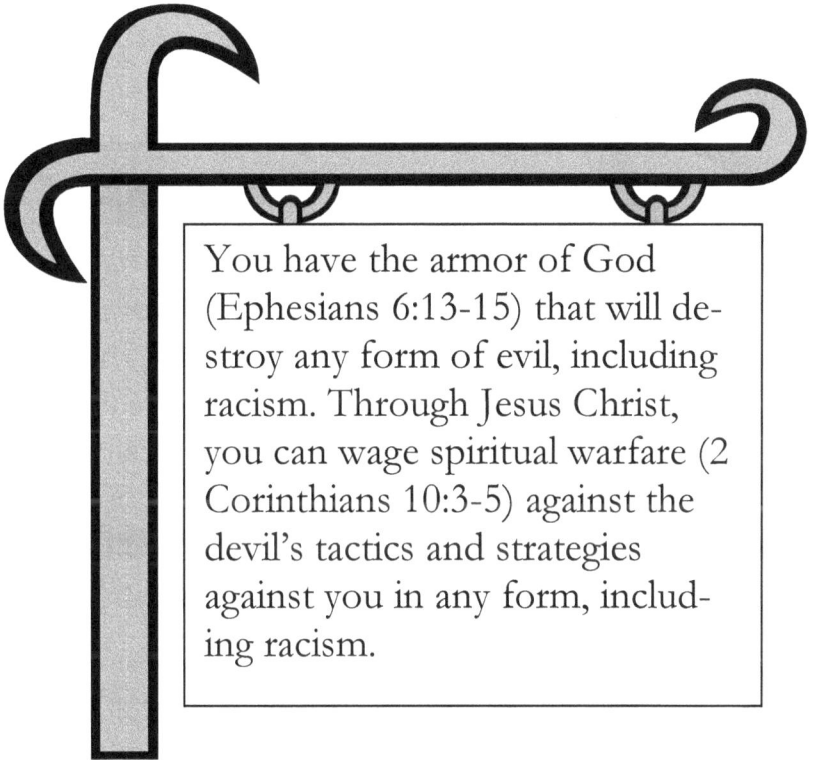

You have the armor of God (Ephesians 6:13-15) that will destroy any form of evil, including racism. Through Jesus Christ, you can wage spiritual warfare (2 Corinthians 10:3-5) against the devil's tactics and strategies against you in any form, including racism.

110

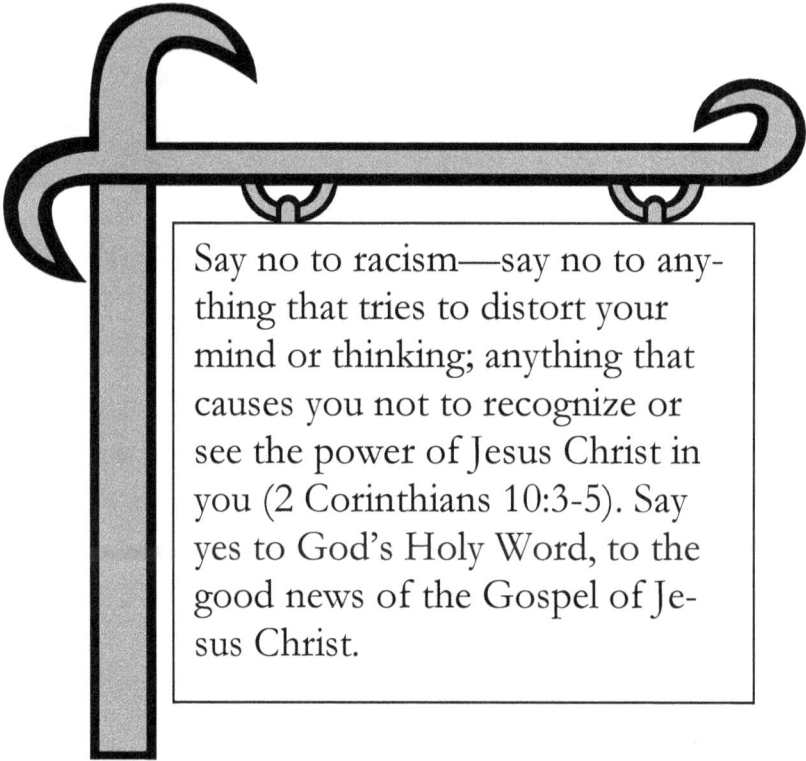

Say no to racism—say no to anything that tries to distort your mind or thinking; anything that causes you not to recognize or see the power of Jesus Christ in you (2 Corinthians 10:3-5). Say yes to God's Holy Word, to the good news of the Gospel of Jesus Christ.

111

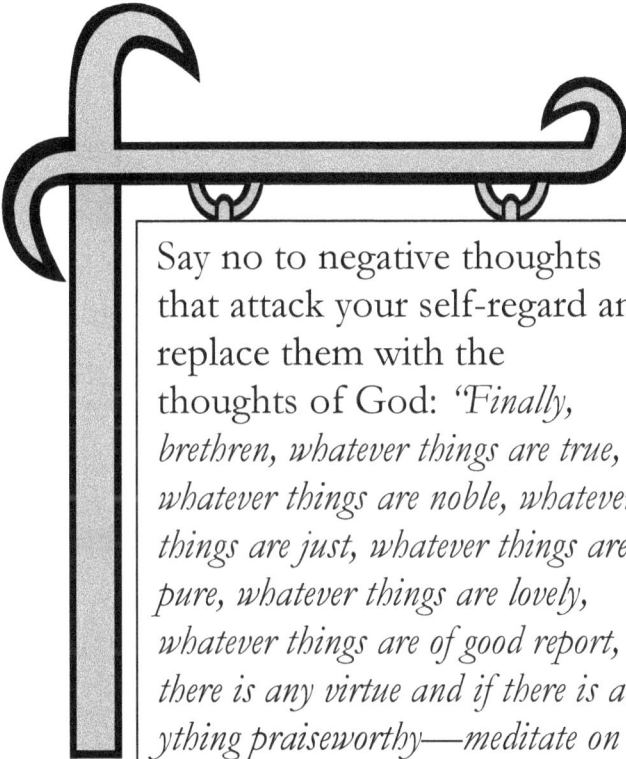

Say no to negative thoughts that attack your self-regard and replace them with the thoughts of God: *"Finally, brethren, whatever things are true, whatever things are noble, whatever things are just, whatever things are pure, whatever things are lovely, whatever things are of good report, if there is any virtue and if there is anything praiseworthy—meditate on these things."* (Philippians 4:8) Say no to racism!

112

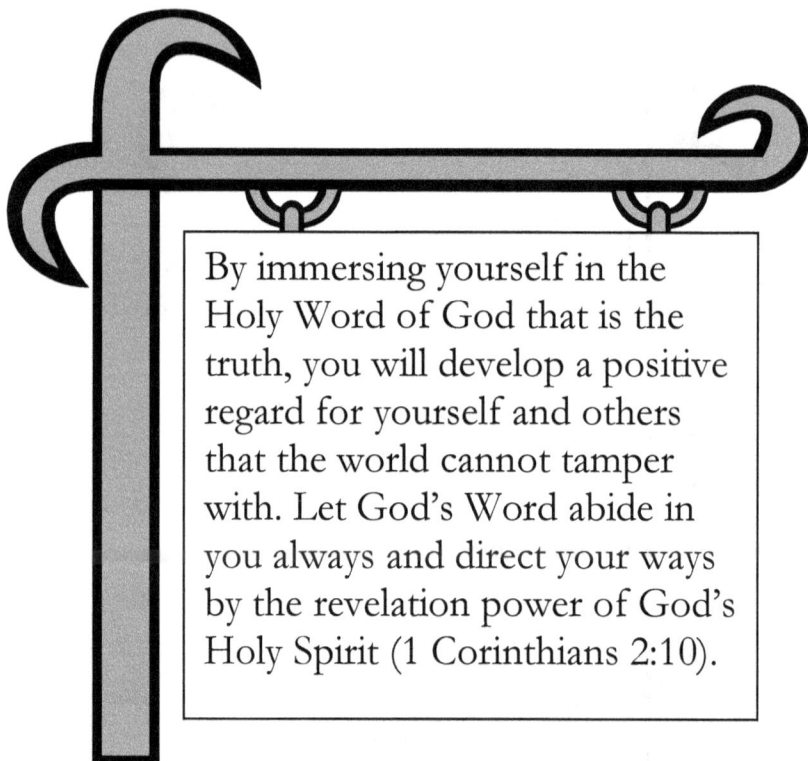

By immersing yourself in the Holy Word of God that is the truth, you will develop a positive regard for yourself and others that the world cannot tamper with. Let God's Word abide in you always and direct your ways by the revelation power of God's Holy Spirit (1 Corinthians 2:10).

113

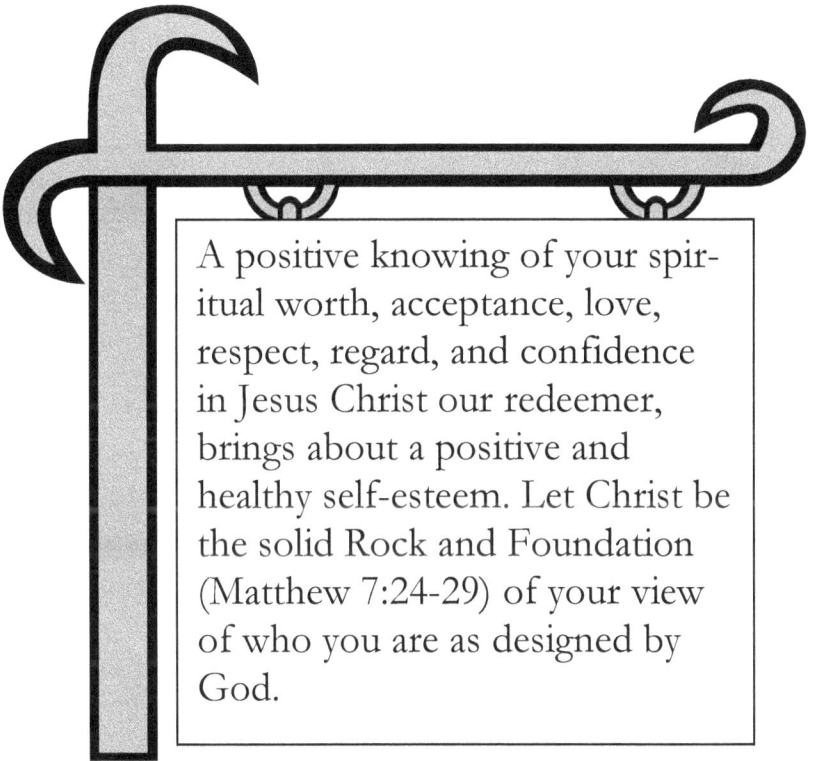

A positive knowing of your spiritual worth, acceptance, love, respect, regard, and confidence in Jesus Christ our redeemer, brings about a positive and healthy self-esteem. Let Christ be the solid Rock and Foundation (Matthew 7:24-29) of your view of who you are as designed by God.

114

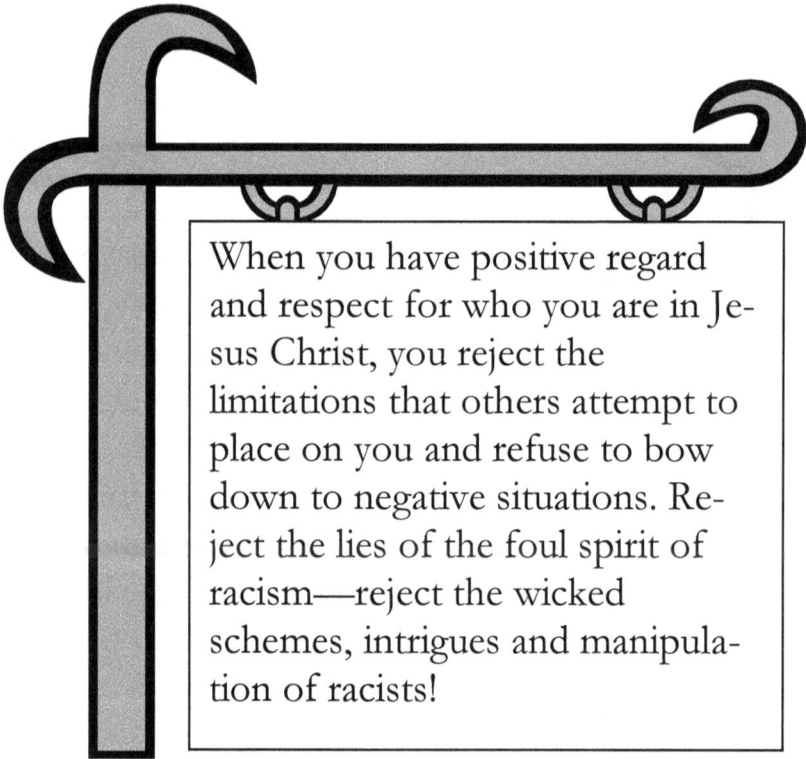

When you have positive regard and respect for who you are in Jesus Christ, you reject the limitations that others attempt to place on you and refuse to bow down to negative situations. Reject the lies of the foul spirit of racism—reject the wicked schemes, intrigues and manipulation of racists!

115

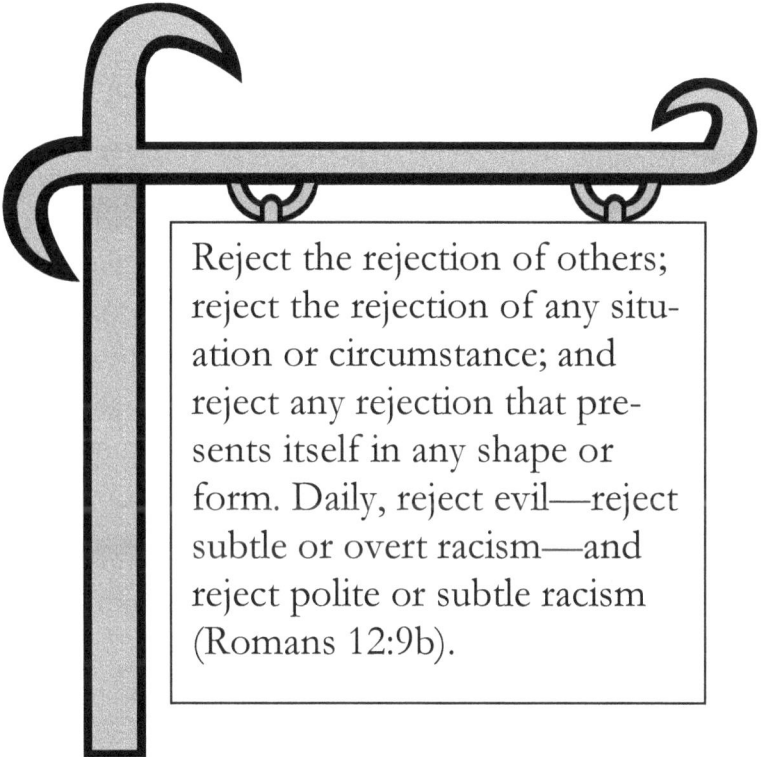

Reject the rejection of others; reject the rejection of any situation or circumstance; and reject any rejection that presents itself in any shape or form. Daily, reject evil—reject subtle or overt racism—and reject polite or subtle racism (Romans 12:9b).

116

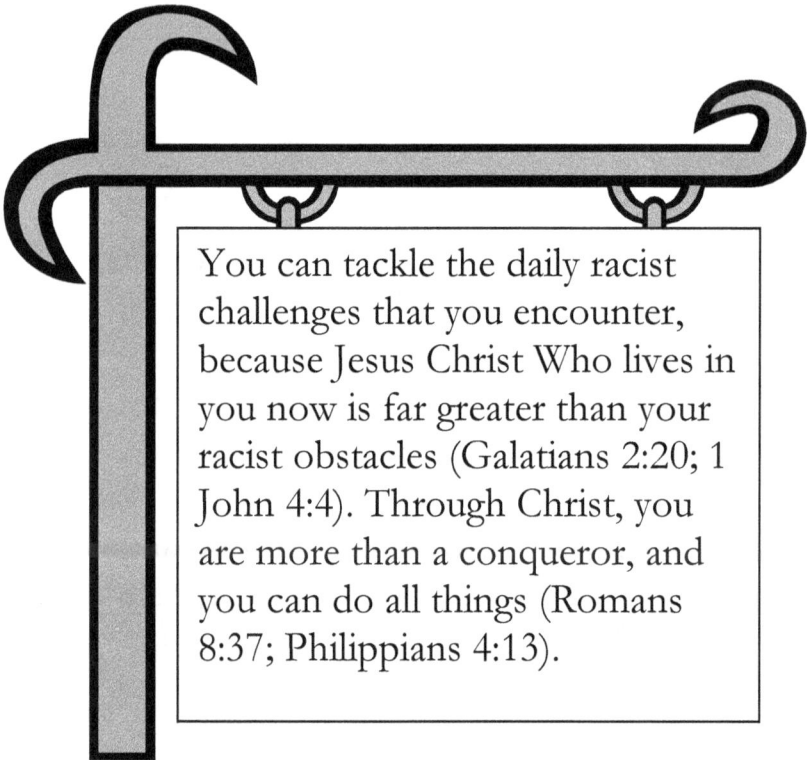

You can tackle the daily racist challenges that you encounter, because Jesus Christ Who lives in you now is far greater than your racist obstacles (Galatians 2:20; 1 John 4:4). Through Christ, you are more than a conqueror, and you can do all things (Romans 8:37; Philippians 4:13).

117

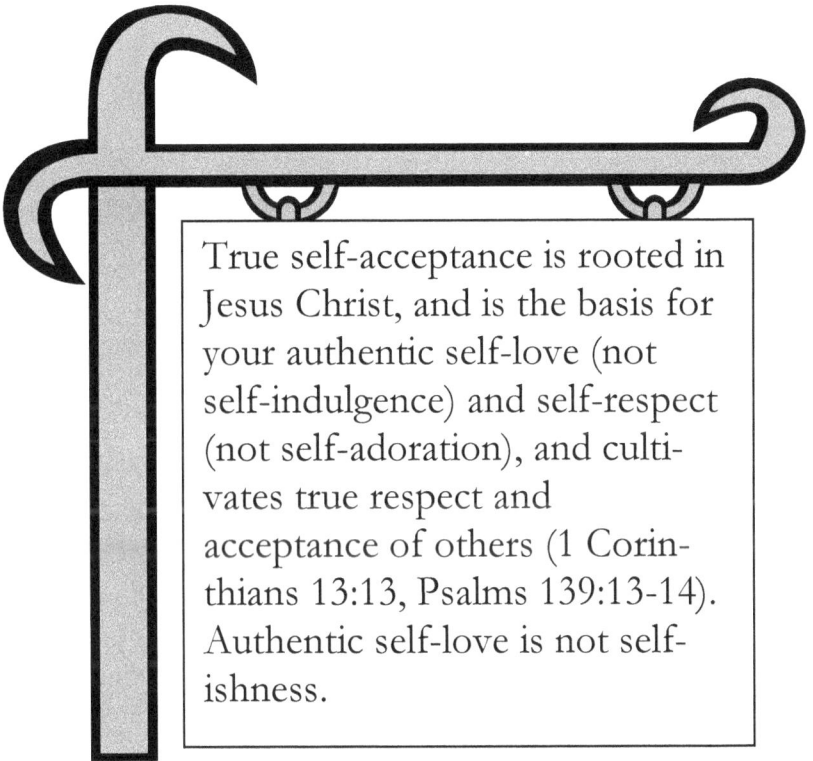

True self-acceptance is rooted in Jesus Christ, and is the basis for your authentic self-love (not self-indulgence) and self-respect (not self-adoration), and cultivates true respect and acceptance of others (1 Corinthians 13:13, Psalms 139:13-14). Authentic self-love is not selfishness.

118

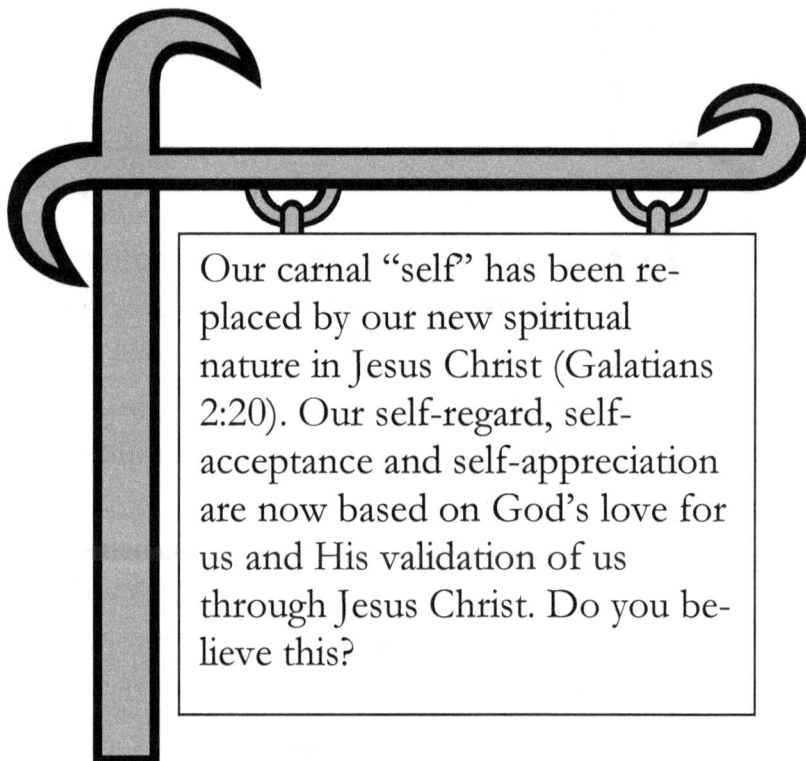

Our carnal "self" has been re-placed by our new spiritual nature in Jesus Christ (Galatians 2:20). Our self-regard, self-acceptance and self-appreciation are now based on God's love for us and His validation of us through Jesus Christ. Do you be-lieve this?

119

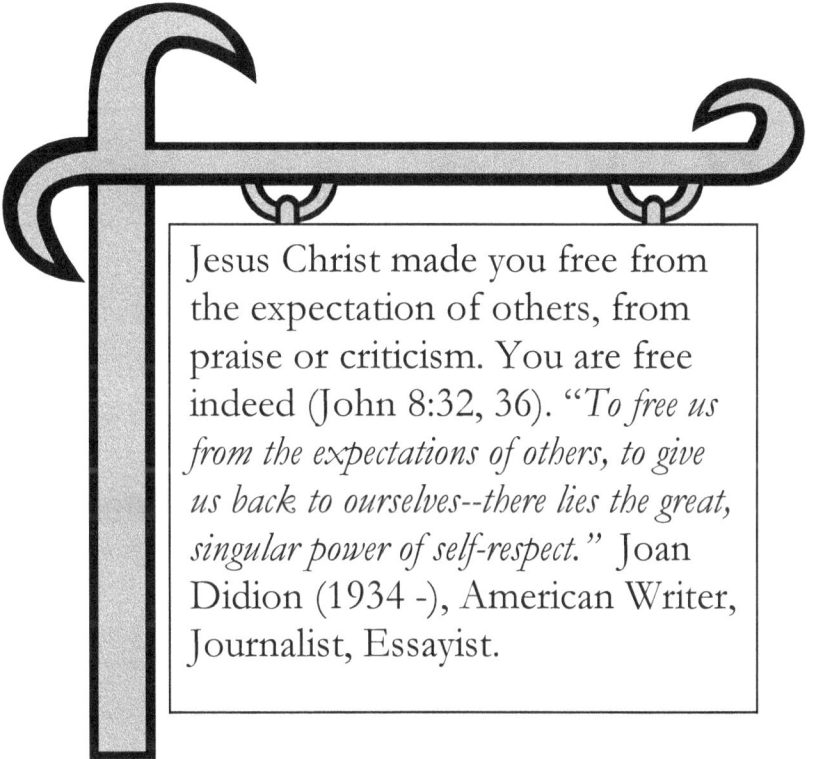

Jesus Christ made you free from the expectation of others, from praise or criticism. You are free indeed (John 8:32, 36). *"To free us from the expectations of others, to give us back to ourselves--there lies the great, singular power of self-respect."* Joan Didion (1934 -), American Writer, Journalist, Essayist.

120

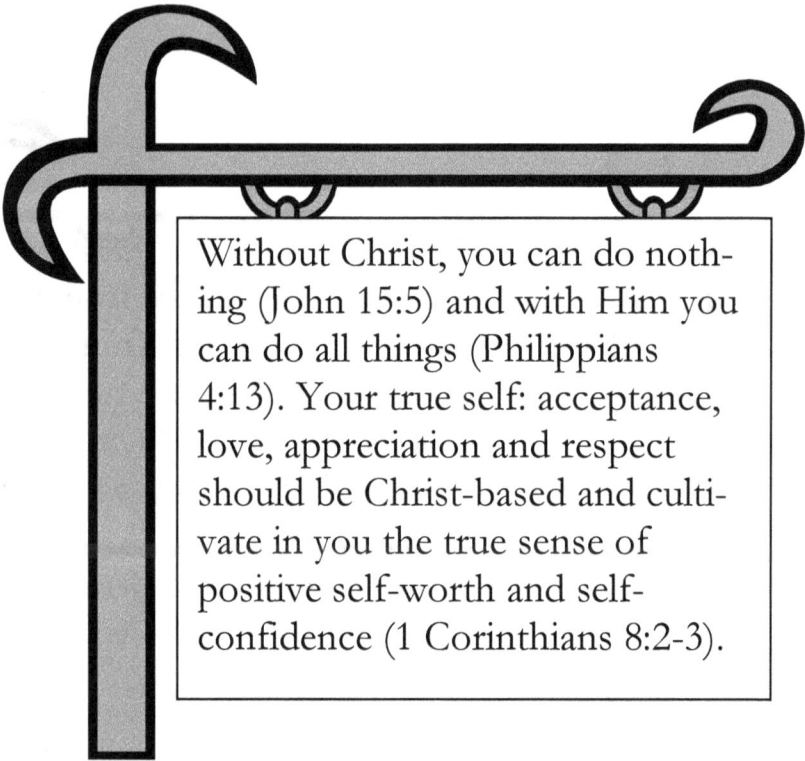

Without Christ, you can do nothing (John 15:5) and with Him you can do all things (Philippians 4:13). Your true self: acceptance, love, appreciation and respect should be Christ-based and cultivate in you the true sense of positive self-worth and self-confidence (1 Corinthians 8:2-3).

121

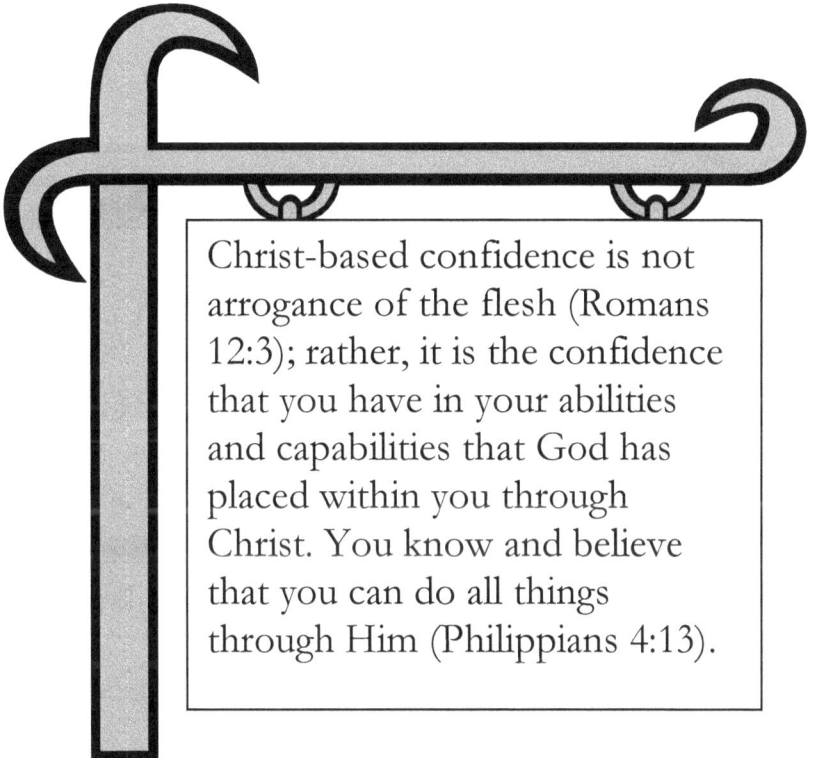

Christ-based confidence is not arrogance of the flesh (Romans 12:3); rather, it is the confidence that you have in your abilities and capabilities that God has placed within you through Christ. You know and believe that you can do all things through Him (Philippians 4:13).

122

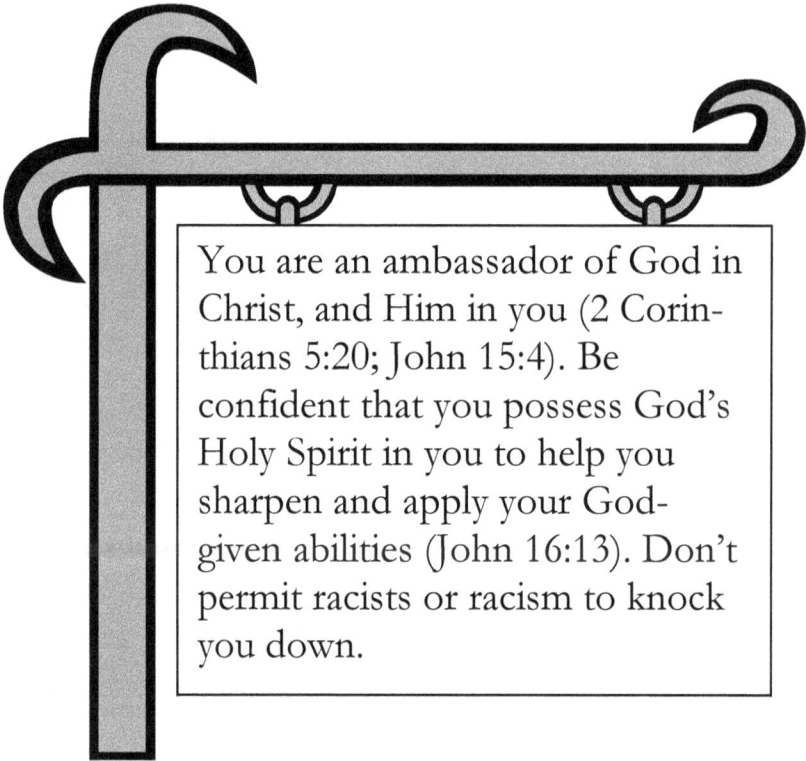

You are an ambassador of God in Christ, and Him in you (2 Corinthians 5:20; John 15:4). Be confident that you possess God's Holy Spirit in you to help you sharpen and apply your God-given abilities (John 16:13). Don't permit racists or racism to knock you down.

123

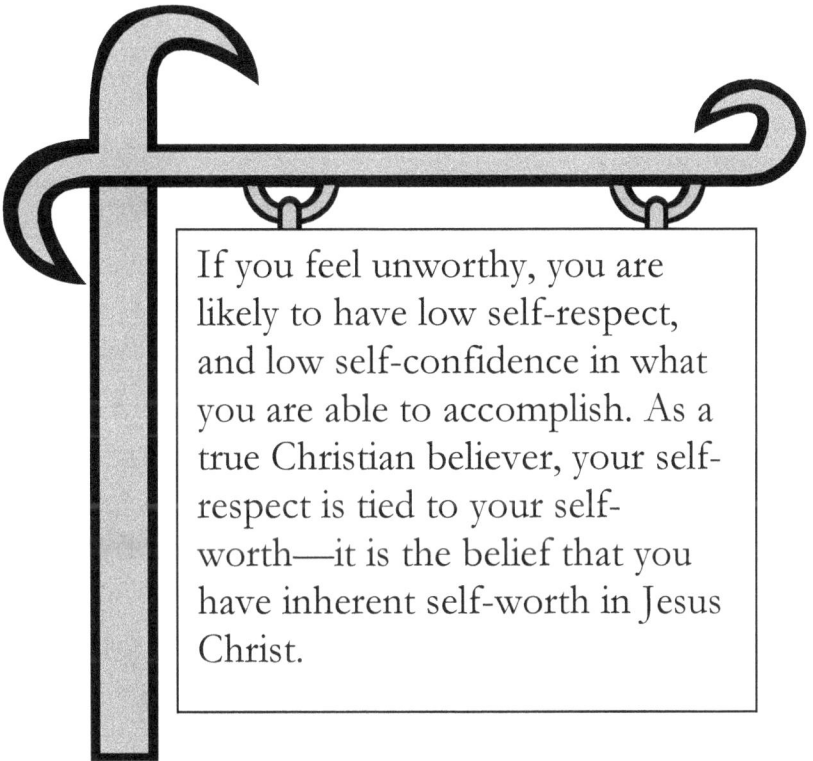

If you feel unworthy, you are likely to have low self-respect, and low self-confidence in what you are able to accomplish. As a true Christian believer, your self-respect is tied to your self-worth—it is the belief that you have inherent self-worth in Jesus Christ.

124

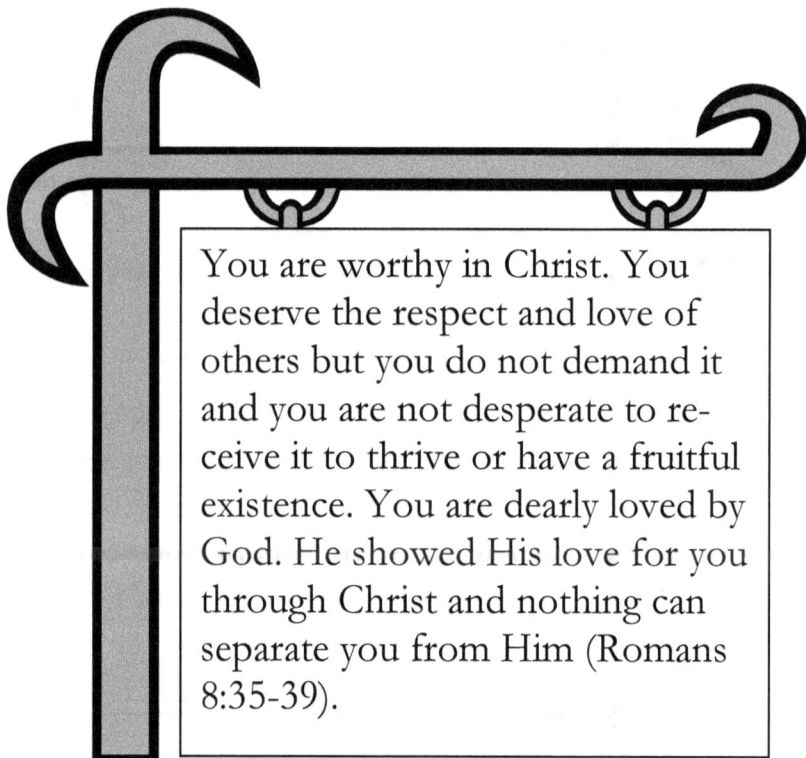

You are worthy in Christ. You deserve the respect and love of others but you do not demand it and you are not desperate to receive it to thrive or have a fruitful existence. You are dearly loved by God. He showed His love for you through Christ and nothing can separate you from Him (Romans 8:35-39).

125

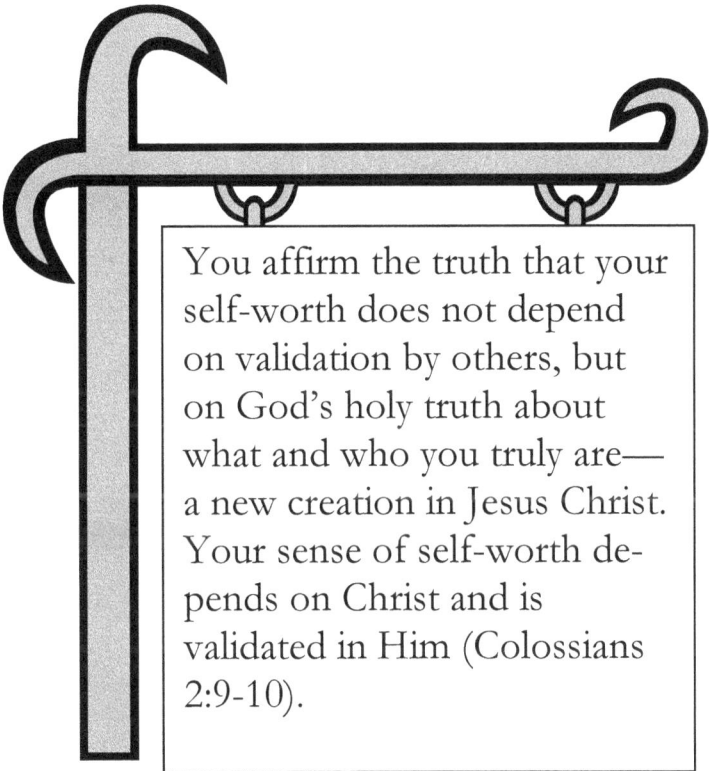

You affirm the truth that your self-worth does not depend on validation by others, but on God's holy truth about what and who you truly are— a new creation in Jesus Christ. Your sense of self-worth depends on Christ and is validated in Him (Colossians 2:9-10).

126

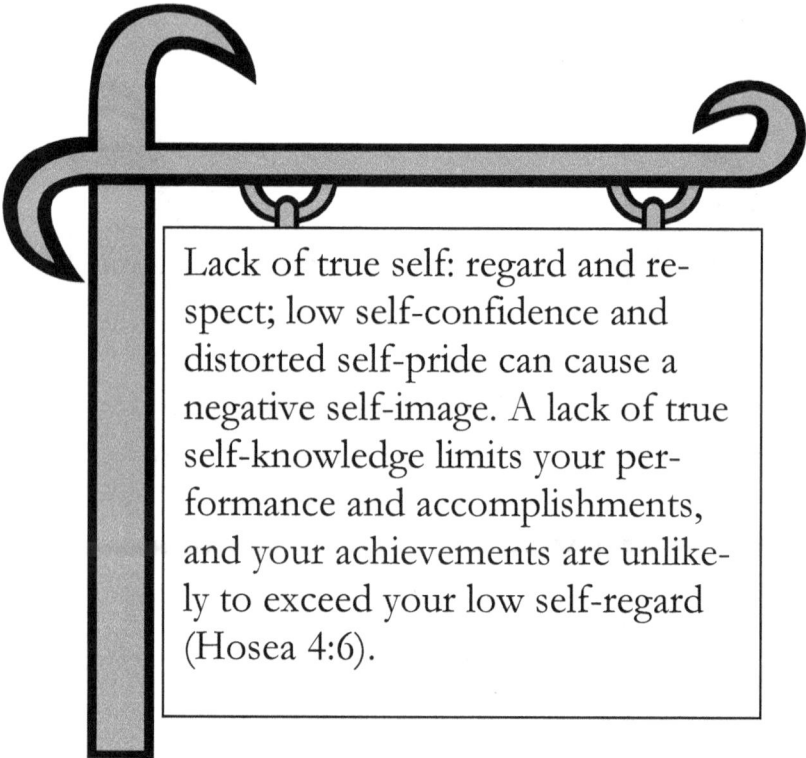

Lack of true self: regard and respect; low self-confidence and distorted self-pride can cause a negative self-image. A lack of true self-knowledge limits your performance and accomplishments, and your achievements are unlikely to exceed your low self-regard (Hosea 4:6).

127

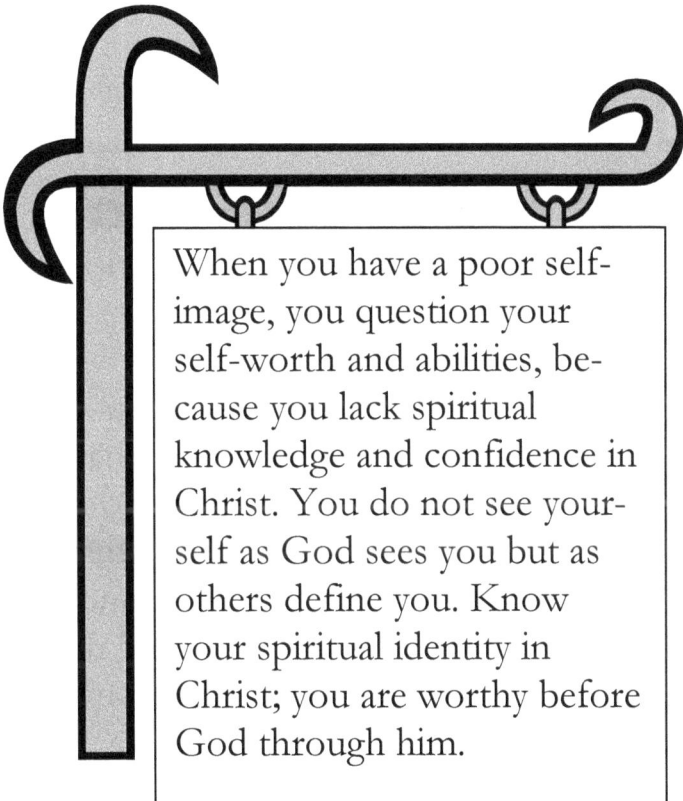

When you have a poor self-image, you question your self-worth and abilities, because you lack spiritual knowledge and confidence in Christ. You do not see yourself as God sees you but as others define you. Know your spiritual identity in Christ; you are worthy before God through him.

128

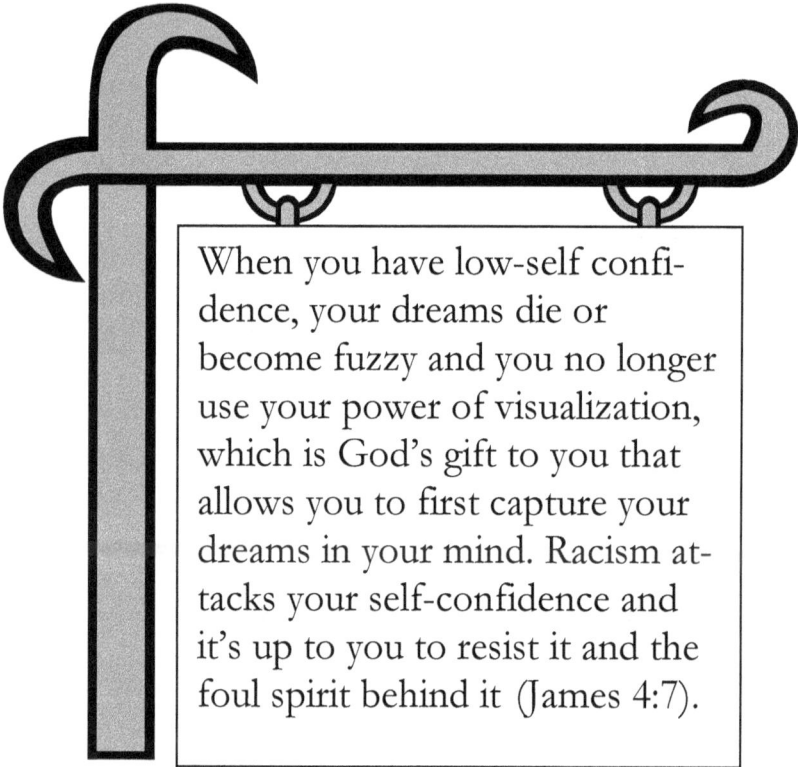

When you have low-self confidence, your dreams die or become fuzzy and you no longer use your power of visualization, which is God's gift to you that allows you to first capture your dreams in your mind. Racism attacks your self-confidence and it's up to you to resist it and the foul spirit behind it (James 4:7).

129

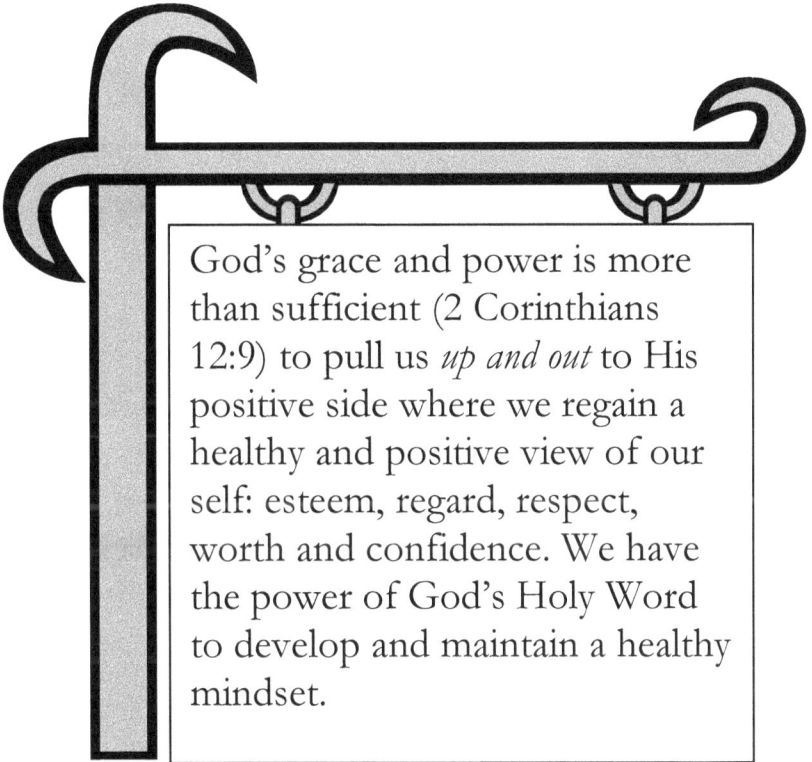

God's grace and power is more than sufficient (2 Corinthians 12:9) to pull us *up and out* to His positive side where we regain a healthy and positive view of our self: esteem, regard, respect, worth and confidence. We have the power of God's Holy Word to develop and maintain a healthy mindset.

130

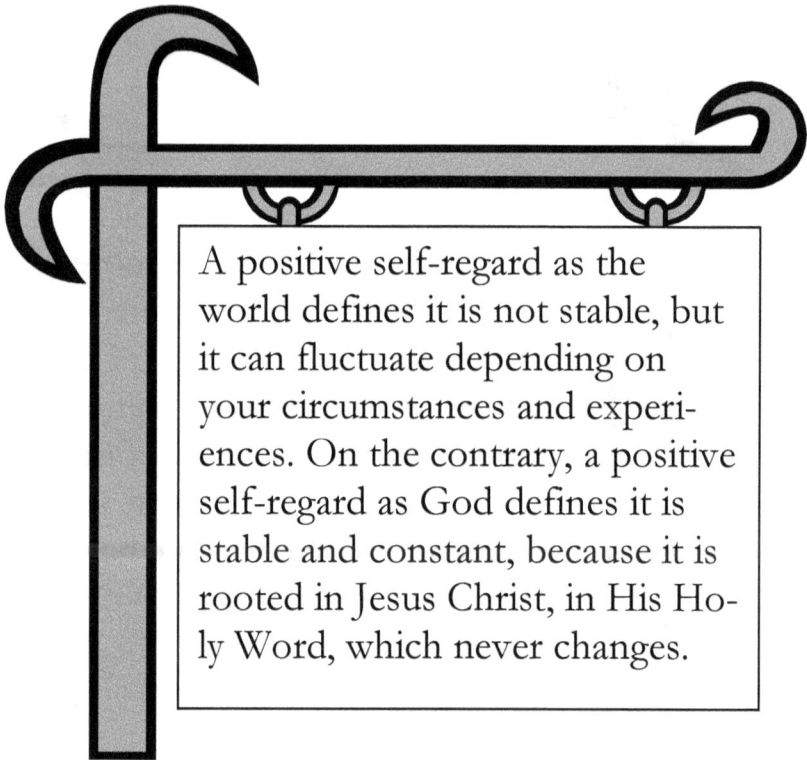

A positive self-regard as the world defines it is not stable, but it can fluctuate depending on your circumstances and experiences. On the contrary, a positive self-regard as God defines it is stable and constant, because it is rooted in Jesus Christ, in His Holy Word, which never changes.

131

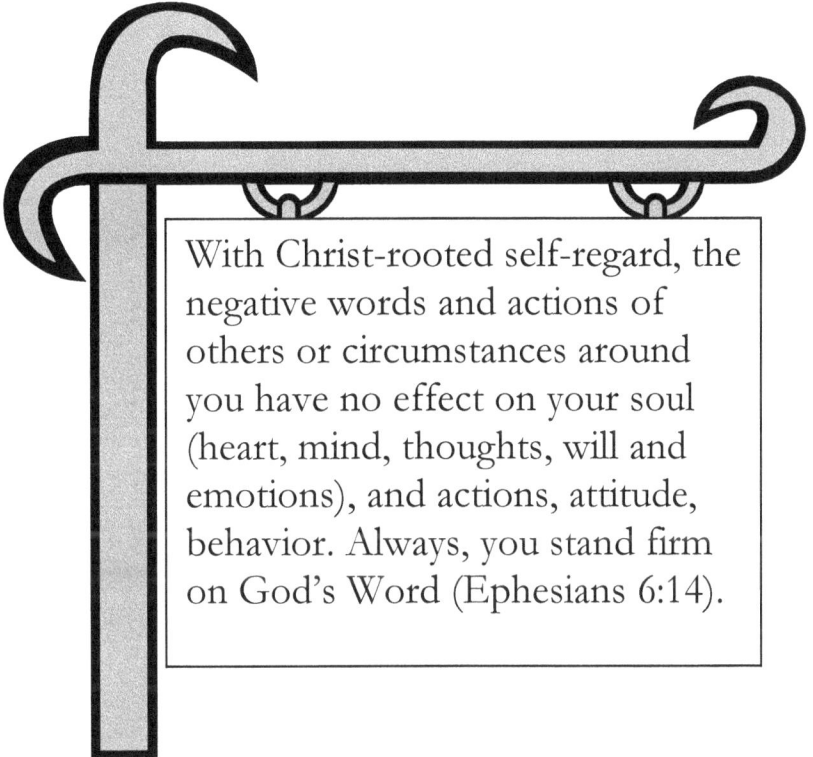

With Christ-rooted self-regard, the negative words and actions of others or circumstances around you have no effect on your soul (heart, mind, thoughts, will and emotions), and actions, attitude, behavior. Always, you stand firm on God's Word (Ephesians 6:14).

132

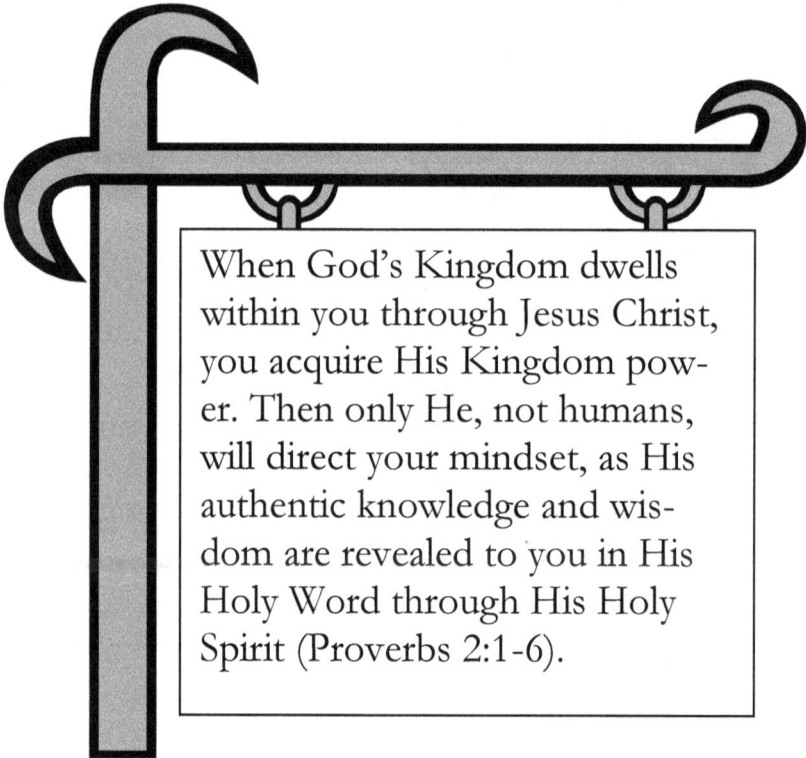

When God's Kingdom dwells within you through Jesus Christ, you acquire His Kingdom power. Then only He, not humans, will direct your mindset, as His authentic knowledge and wisdom are revealed to you in His Holy Word through His Holy Spirit (Proverbs 2:1-6).

133

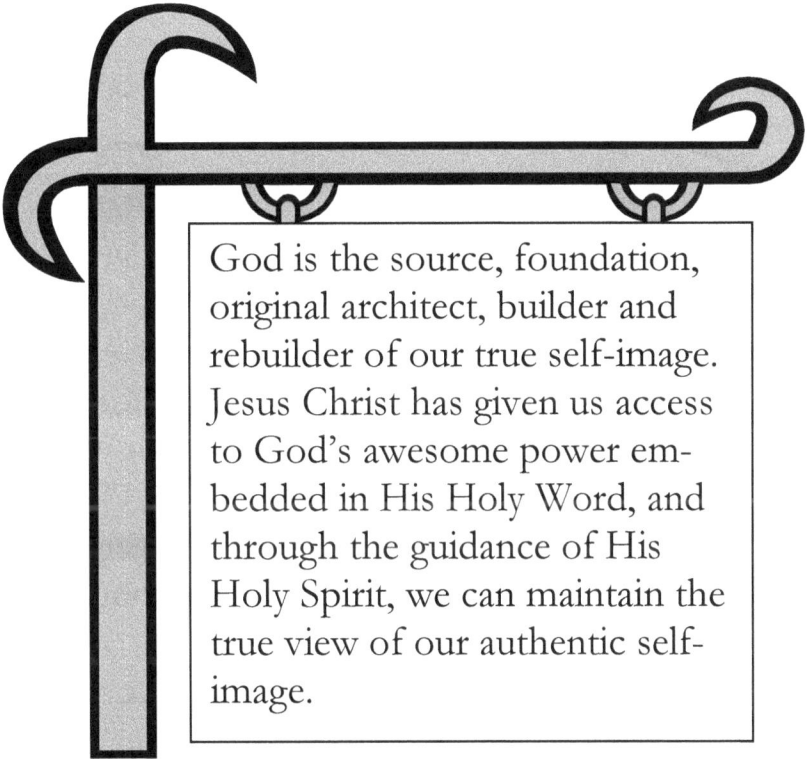

God is the source, foundation, original architect, builder and rebuilder of our true self-image. Jesus Christ has given us access to God's awesome power embedded in His Holy Word, and through the guidance of His Holy Spirit, we can maintain the true view of our authentic self-image.

134

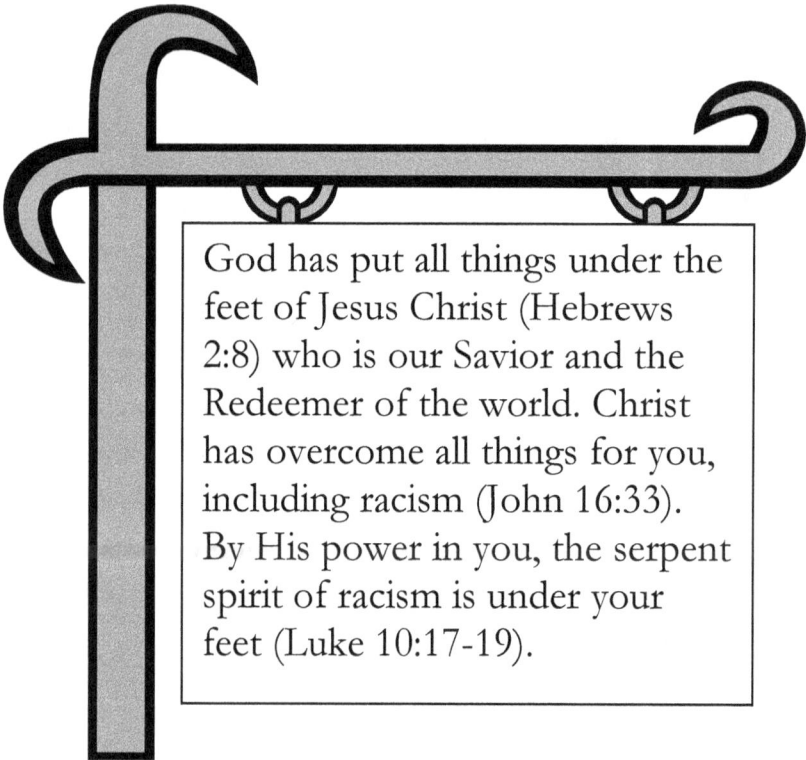

God has put all things under the feet of Jesus Christ (Hebrews 2:8) who is our Savior and the Redeemer of the world. Christ has overcome all things for you, including racism (John 16:33). By His power in you, the serpent spirit of racism is under your feet (Luke 10:17-19).

135

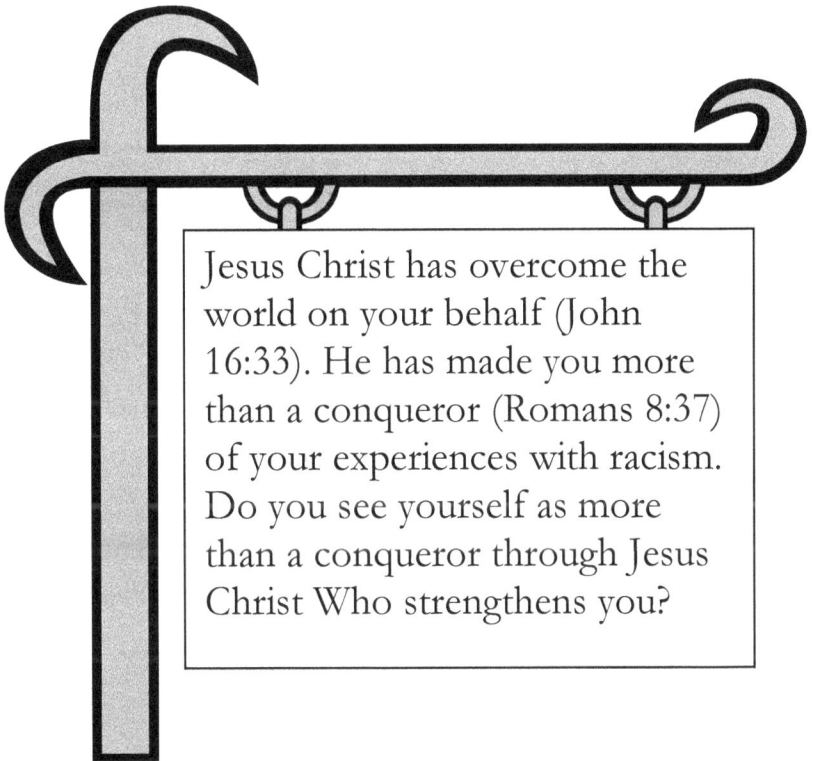

Jesus Christ has overcome the world on your behalf (John 16:33). He has made you more than a conqueror (Romans 8:37) of your experiences with racism. Do you see yourself as more than a conqueror through Jesus Christ Who strengthens you?

136

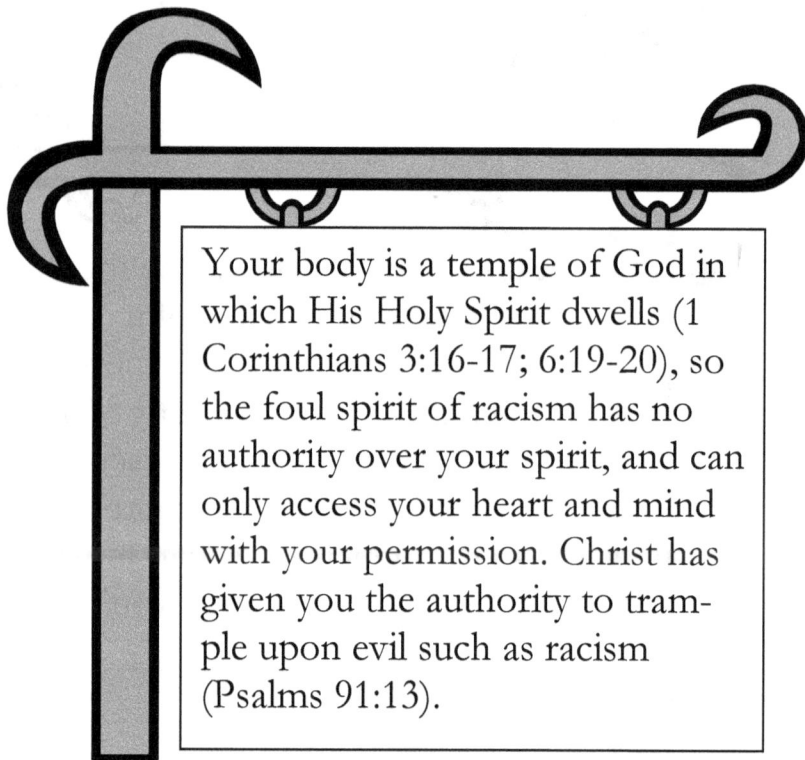

Your body is a temple of God in which His Holy Spirit dwells (1 Corinthians 3:16-17; 6:19-20), so the foul spirit of racism has no authority over your spirit, and can only access your heart and mind with your permission. Christ has given you the authority to trample upon evil such as racism (Psalms 91:13).

137

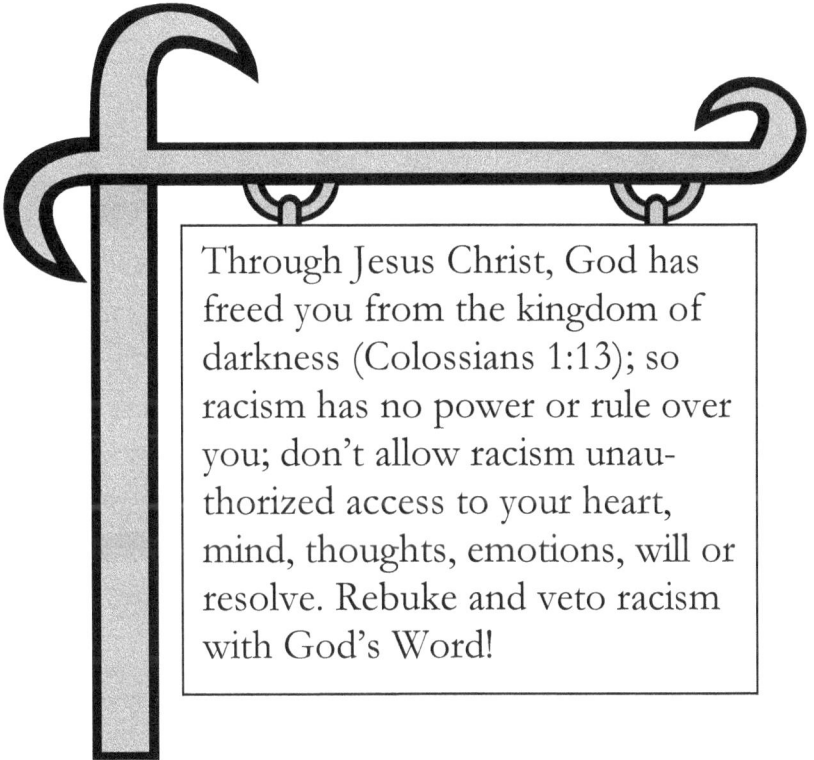

Through Jesus Christ, God has freed you from the kingdom of darkness (Colossians 1:13); so racism has no power or rule over you; don't allow racism unauthorized access to your heart, mind, thoughts, emotions, will or resolve. Rebuke and veto racism with God's Word!

138

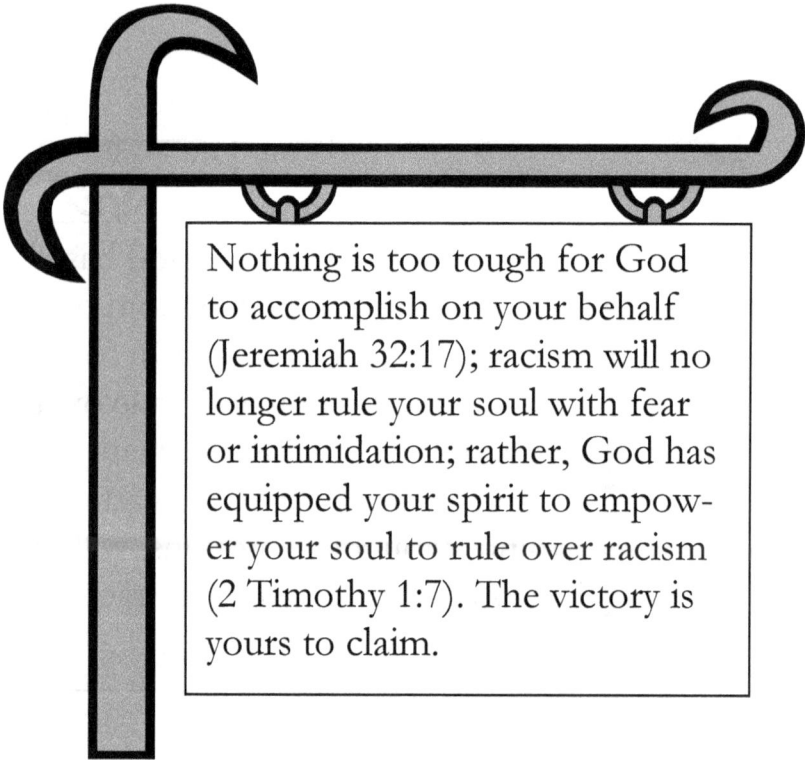

Nothing is too tough for God to accomplish on your behalf (Jeremiah 32:17); racism will no longer rule your soul with fear or intimidation; rather, God has equipped your spirit to empower your soul to rule over racism (2 Timothy 1:7). The victory is yours to claim.

139

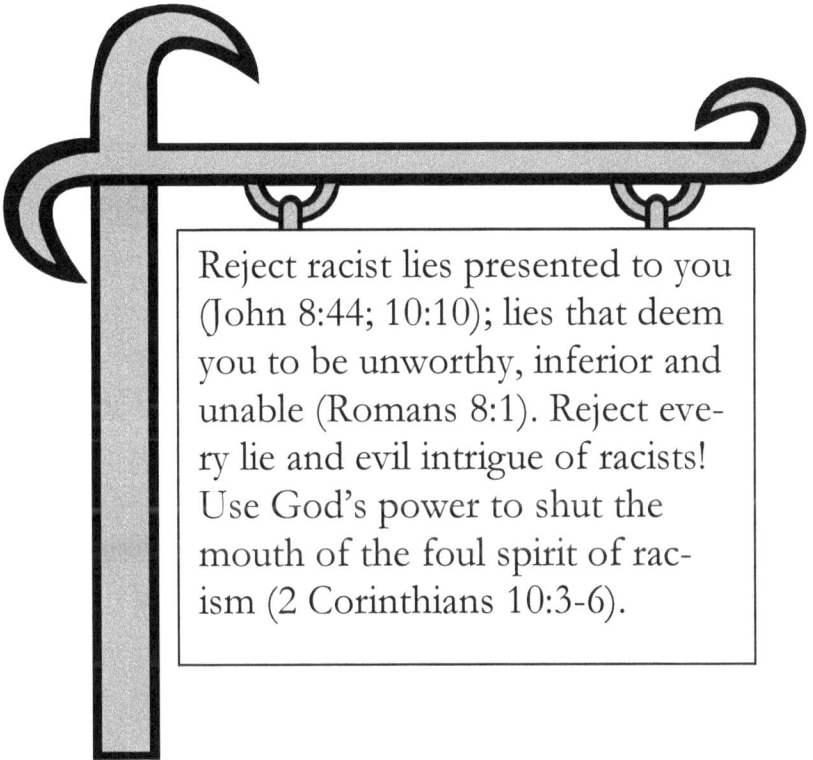

Reject racist lies presented to you (John 8:44; 10:10); lies that deem you to be unworthy, inferior and unable (Romans 8:1). Reject every lie and evil intrigue of racists! Use God's power to shut the mouth of the foul spirit of racism (2 Corinthians 10:3-6).

140

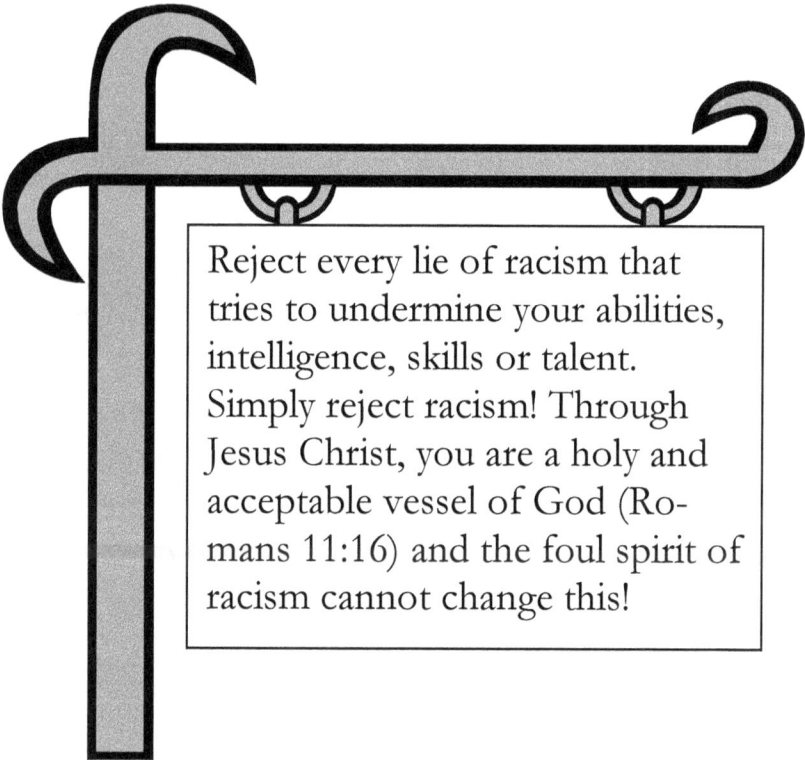

Reject every lie of racism that tries to undermine your abilities, intelligence, skills or talent. Simply reject racism! Through Jesus Christ, you are a holy and acceptable vessel of God (Romans 11:16) and the foul spirit of racism cannot change this!

141

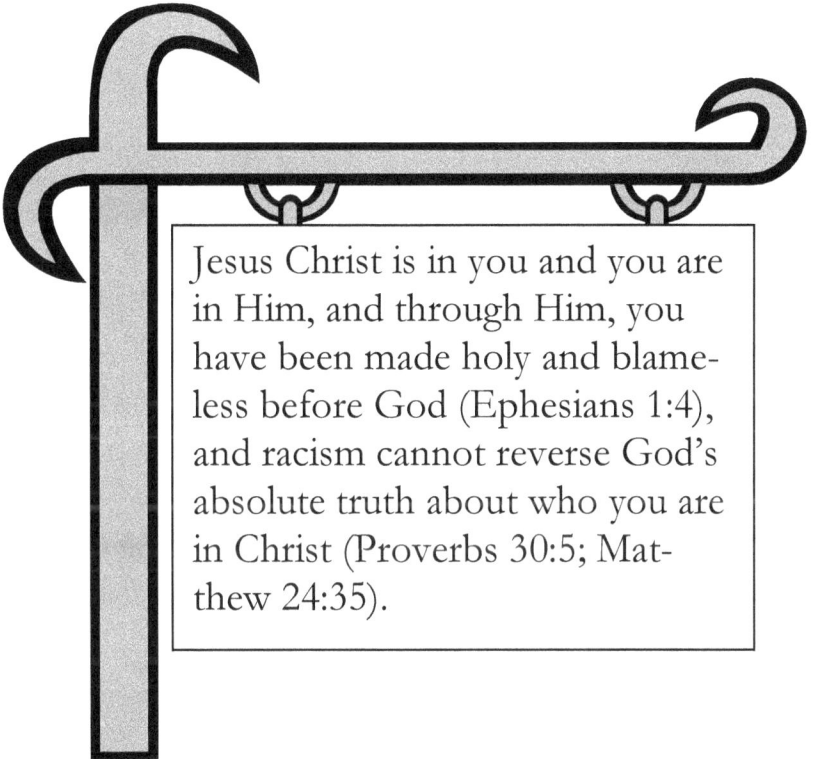

Jesus Christ is in you and you are in Him, and through Him, you have been made holy and blameless before God (Ephesians 1:4), and racism cannot reverse God's absolute truth about who you are in Christ (Proverbs 30:5; Matthew 24:35).

142

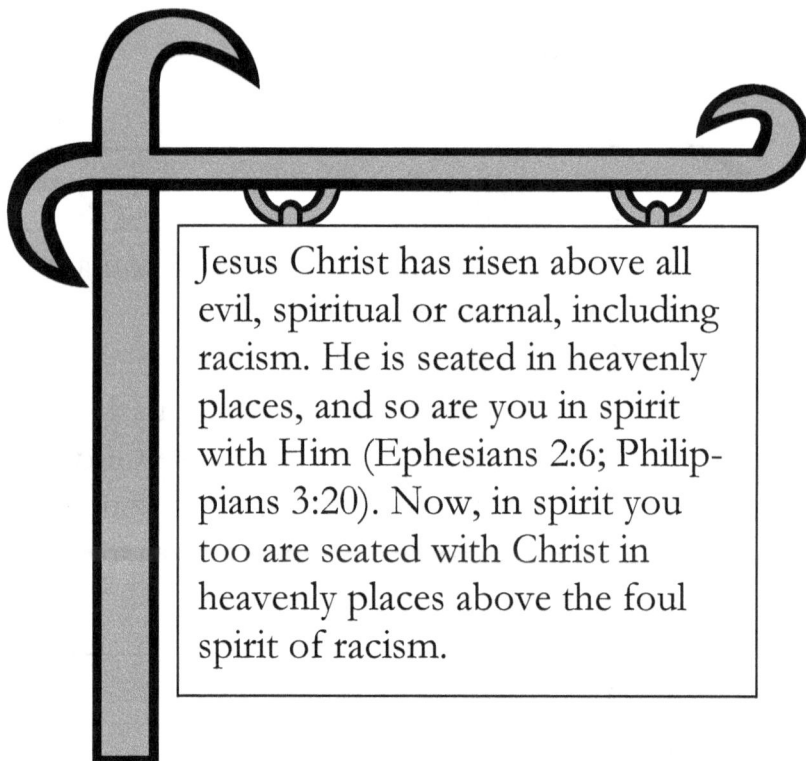

Jesus Christ has risen above all evil, spiritual or carnal, including racism. He is seated in heavenly places, and so are you in spirit with Him (Ephesians 2:6; Philippians 3:20). Now, in spirit you too are seated with Christ in heavenly places above the foul spirit of racism.

143

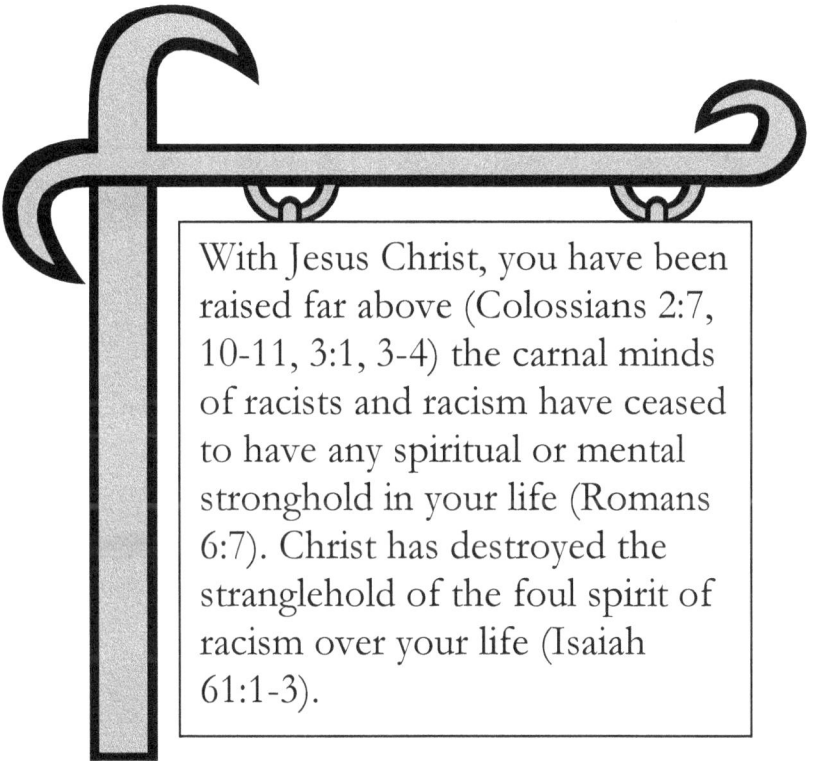

With Jesus Christ, you have been raised far above (Colossians 2:7, 10-11, 3:1, 3-4) the carnal minds of racists and racism have ceased to have any spiritual or mental stronghold in your life (Romans 6:7). Christ has destroyed the stranglehold of the foul spirit of racism over your life (Isaiah 61:1-3).

144

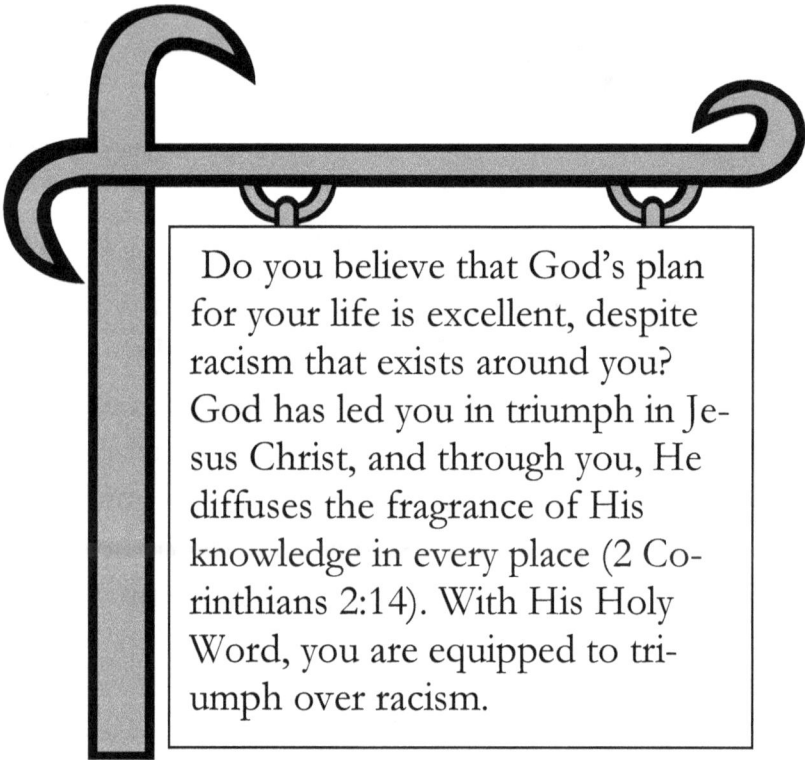

Do you believe that God's plan for your life is excellent, despite racism that exists around you? God has led you in triumph in Jesus Christ, and through you, He diffuses the fragrance of His knowledge in every place (2 Corinthians 2:14). With His Holy Word, you are equipped to triumph over racism.

145

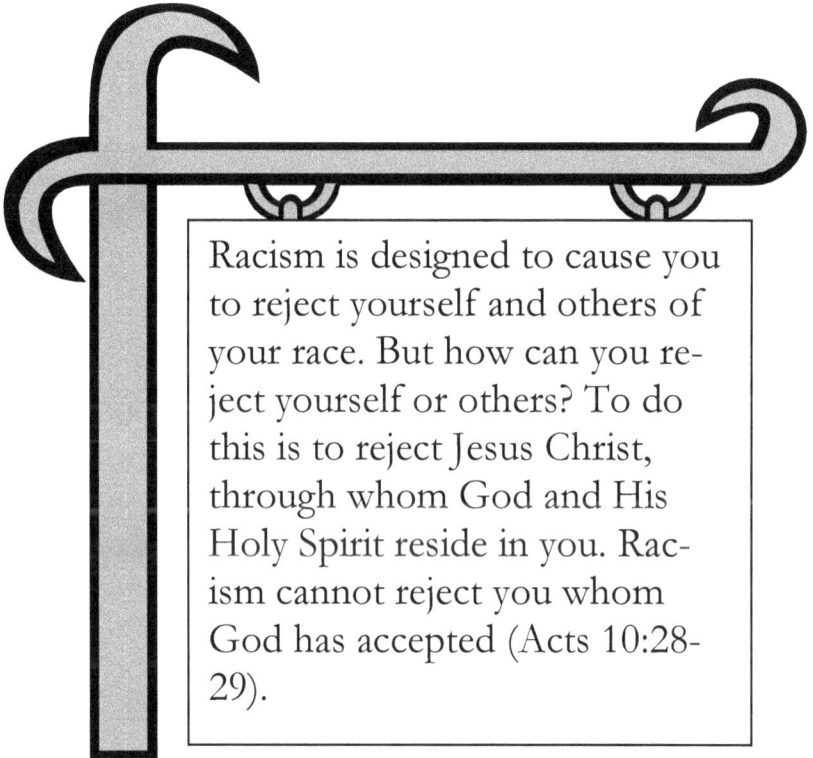

Racism is designed to cause you to reject yourself and others of your race. But how can you reject yourself or others? To do this is to reject Jesus Christ, through whom God and His Holy Spirit reside in you. Racism cannot reject you whom God has accepted (Acts 10:28-29).

146

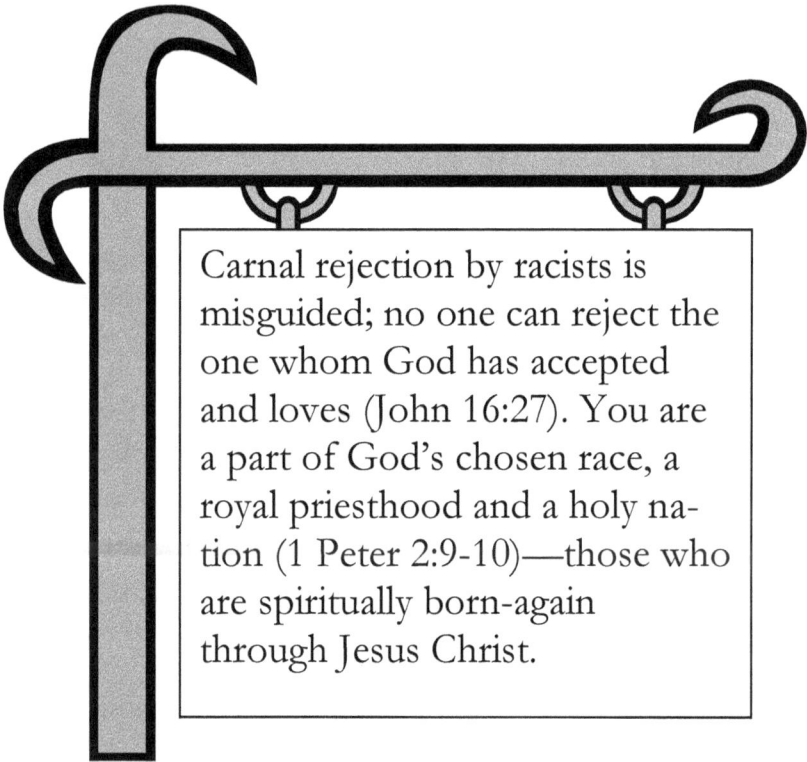

Carnal rejection by racists is misguided; no one can reject the one whom God has accepted and loves (John 16:27). You are a part of God's chosen race, a royal priesthood and a holy nation (1 Peter 2:9-10)—those who are spiritually born-again through Jesus Christ.

147

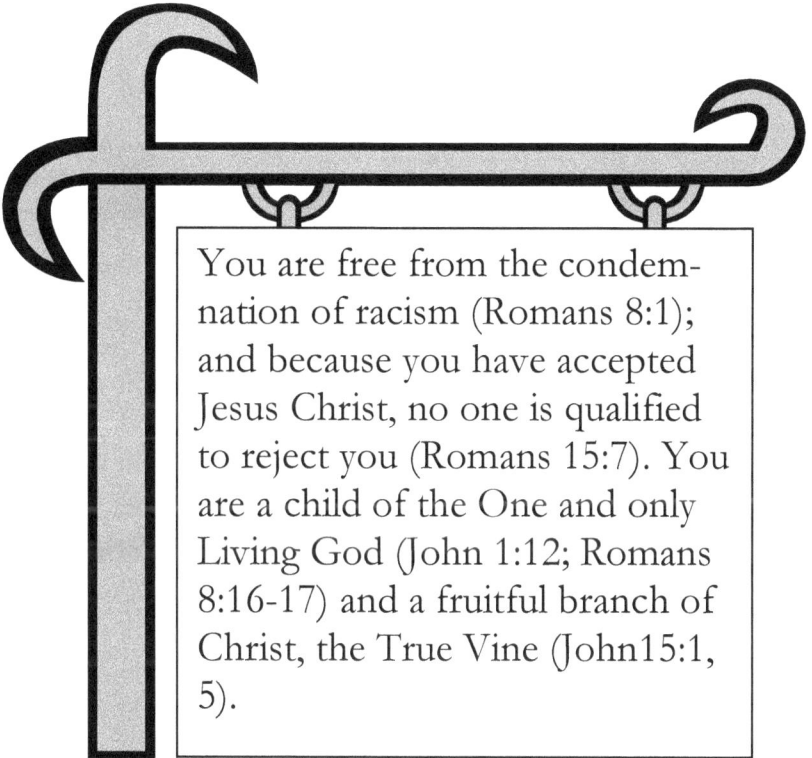

You are free from the condemnation of racism (Romans 8:1); and because you have accepted Jesus Christ, no one is qualified to reject you (Romans 15:7). You are a child of the One and only Living God (John 1:12; Romans 8:16-17) and a fruitful branch of Christ, the True Vine (John15:1, 5).

148

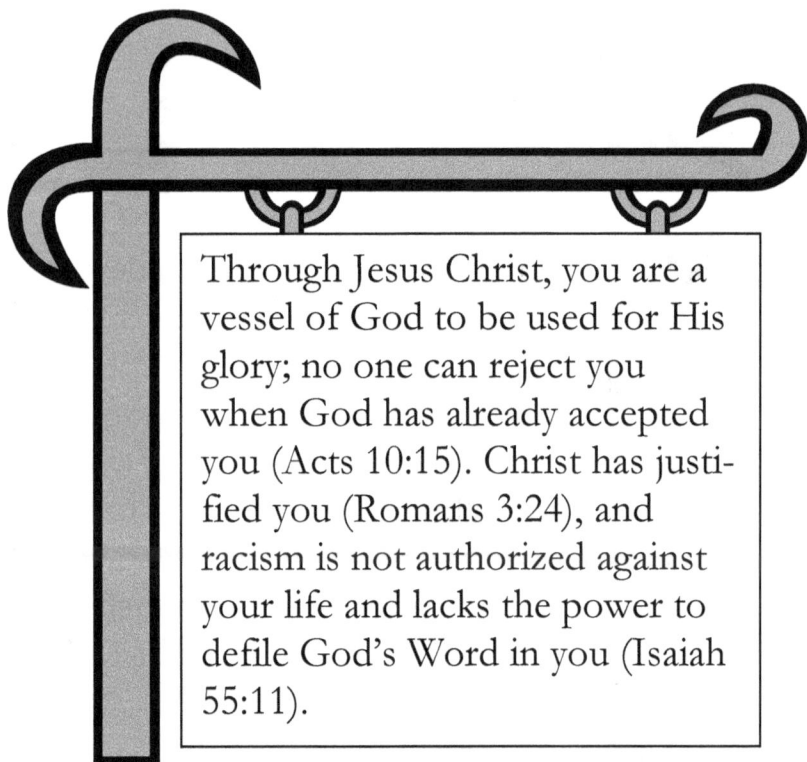

Through Jesus Christ, you are a vessel of God to be used for His glory; no one can reject you when God has already accepted you (Acts 10:15). Christ has justified you (Romans 3:24), and racism is not authorized against your life and lacks the power to defile God's Word in you (Isaiah 55:11).

149

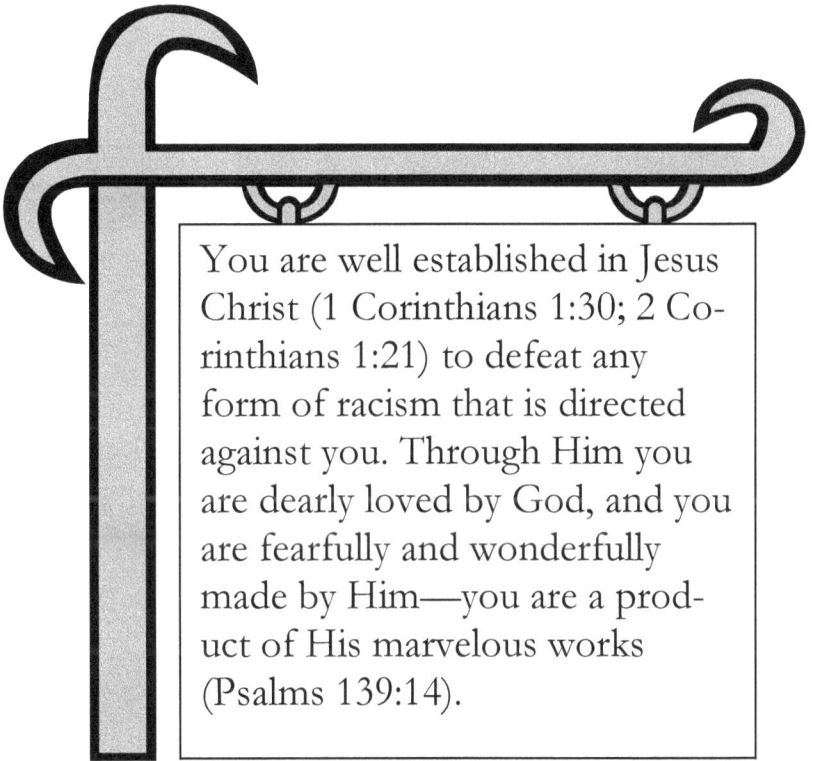

You are well established in Jesus Christ (1 Corinthians 1:30; 2 Corinthians 1:21) to defeat any form of racism that is directed against you. Through Him you are dearly loved by God, and you are fearfully and wonderfully made by Him—you are a product of His marvelous works (Psalms 139:14).

150

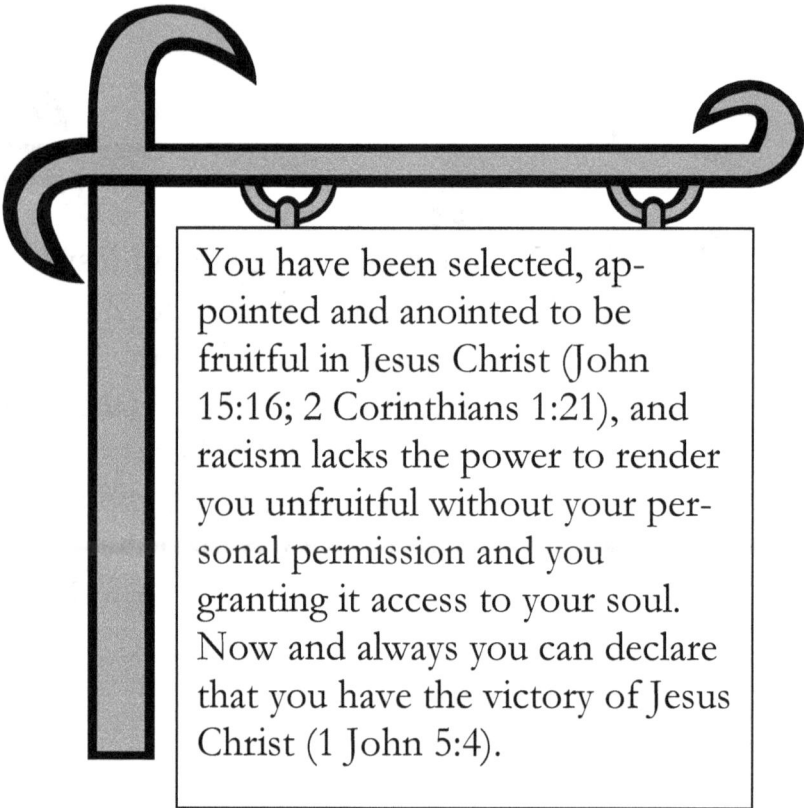

You have been selected, appointed and anointed to be fruitful in Jesus Christ (John 15:16; 2 Corinthians 1:21), and racism lacks the power to render you unfruitful without your personal permission and you granting it access to your soul. Now and always you can declare that you have the victory of Jesus Christ (1 John 5:4).

Available:
RAYS OF VICTORY SERIES

This Book:

150 SIGN POSTS TO VICTORY OVER RACISM
(Volume 3)

Empowering Sign Posts for Victory Over Racism

∞∞∞∞∞∞∞∞ ♦ ♦ ♦ ♦ ∞∞∞∞∞∞∞∞

Excerpts from "Nailing Racism to the Cross"

∞∞∞∞∞∞∞∞ ♦ ♦ ♦ ♦ ∞∞∞∞∞∞∞∞

By
Dr. Jacyee Aniagolu-Johnson

First Paperback Edition
ISBN 978-1-937230-03-6

Also Available:
RAYS OF VICTORY SERIES

150 SIGN POSTS TO VICTORY OVER RACISM
(Volume 1)

Empowering Sign Posts for Victory Over Racism

∞∞∞∞∞∞∞∞∞ ♦ ♦ ♦ ♦ ♦ ∞∞∞∞∞∞∞∞∞

Excerpts from "Nailing Racism to the Cross"

∞∞∞∞∞∞∞∞∞ ♦ ♦ ♦ ♦ ♦ ∞∞∞∞∞∞∞∞∞

By
Dr. Jacyee Aniagolu-Johnson

First Paperback Edition
ISBN 978-1-937230-01-2

RAYS OF VICTORY SERIES

150 SIGN POSTS TO VICTORY OVER RACISM
(Volume 2)

Empowering Sign Posts for Victory Over Racism

∞∞∞∞∞∞∞∞∞ ♦ ♦ ♦ ♦ ♦ ∞∞∞∞∞∞∞∞∞

Excerpts from "Nailing Racism to the Cross"

∞∞∞∞∞∞∞∞∞ ♦ ♦ ♦ ♦ ♦ ∞∞∞∞∞∞∞∞∞

By
Dr. Jacyee Aniagolu-Johnson

First Paperback Edition
ISBN 978-1-937230-02-9

RAYS OF VICTORY SERIES

150 POWER THOUGHTS AGAINST RACISM

Power of a Christ-rooted Mindset Over Racism

∞∞∞∞∞∞∞∞∞∞ ♦ ♦ ♦ ♦ ∞∞∞∞∞∞∞∞∞∞

Readings from Nailing Racism to the Cross"

∞∞∞∞∞∞∞∞∞∞ ♦ ♦ ♦ ♦ ∞∞∞∞∞∞∞∞∞∞

By
Dr. Jacyee Aniagolu-Johnson

First Paperback Edition
ISBN 978-1-937230-00-5

RAYS OF VICTORY SERIES

WORKBOOK SERIES

FOOTPRINTS OF VICTORY OVER RACISM

In the Secret Place With God (Volume 1)

Illuminating Daily Guideposts for God's Rays of Victory Over Racism

By
Dr. Jacyee Aniagolu-Johnson

First Paperback Edition
ISBN 978-0-9789669-5-9

RAYS OF VICTORY SERIES

WORKBOOK SERIES

FOOTPRINTS OF VICTORY OVER RACISM

In the Secret Place With God (Volume 2)

Illuminating Daily Guideposts for God's Rays of Victory Over Racism

By
Dr. Jacyee Aniagolu-Johnson

First Paperback Edition
ISBN 978-0-9789669-6-6

RAYS OF VICTORY SERIES

ON THE HAMMOCK:

WITH THE SWORD OF THE SPIRIT

FOR INDIVIDUAL VICTORY OVER RACISM

A Meditation Journal
[40 Days of Daily Meditation]
(Volume 1)

By
Dr. Jacyee Aniagolu-Johnson

First Paperback Edition
ISBN 978-0-9789669-8-0

RAYS OF VICTORY SERIES

ON THE HAMMOCK:

WITH THE OIL OF GRACE

FOR INDIVIDUAL VICTORY OVER RACISM

A Meditation Journal
[40 Days of Daily Meditation]
(Volume 2)

By
Dr. Jacyee Aniagolu-Johnson

First Paperback Edition
ISBN 978-0-9789669-9-7

RAYS OF VICTORY SERIES

ONE ON ONE WITH GOD

FOR VICTORY OVER RACISM

Daily Prayer Conversations With God for Individual Victory Over Racism

By
Dr. Jacyee Aniagolu-Johnson

First Paperback Edition:
ISBN 978-0-9789669-7-3

RAYS OF VICTORY SERIES

My Rays of Victory

BIBLE STUDY DIARY

A Unique Diary for your Signature Penmanship as you Triumph Over Racism

By
Dr. Jacyee Aniagolu-Johnson

First Paperback Edition:
ISBN: 978-0-9789669-4-2

Rays of Victory Series

Correspondence:

Please send Correspondence to:

Marble Tower Publishing

P.O. Box 1654, Laurel, Maryland 20725

OR

Submit a Contact Request Form at:

www.marbletowerpublishing.com

www.ravbookseries.com

www.ingramcontent.com/pod-product-compliance
Lightning Source LLC
Chambersburg PA
CBHW071122280326
41935CB00010B/1092